Inflation, Exchange Rates,
and the
World Economy

INFLATION EXCHANGE RATES AND THE WORLD ECONOMY

LECTURES ON INTERNATIONAL MONETARY ECONOMICS

THIRD EDITION

W. M. CORDEN

THE UNIVERSITY OF CHICAGO PRESS

The University of Chicago Press, Chicago 60637
Oxford University Press, Walton Street, Oxford OX2 6DP

Printed in Great Britain

95 94 93 92 91 90 89 88 87 86   5 4 3 2 1

ISBN: 0–226–11580–1 (cloth)
ISBN: 0–226–11582–8 (paper)

PREFACE TO THE THIRD EDITION

FOR the third edition I have written three essays, Chapters 11, 12, and 13, that analyse the macro-economic interactions among major O.E.C.D. economies within the current system of flexible exchange rates and capital mobility. They aim to take account of some recent developments in the theory of open-economy macro-economics, including the theory of policy co-ordination, as well as to provide simple expositions of complex subjects.

I have rewritten Chapter 10 on European integration, taking into account the European Monetary System, and have dropped the chapter on the transition to monetary integration. I have also dropped the chapter of 'Afterthoughts' that I wrote for the second edition. I have made some changes in Chapter 9, but otherwise have kept the first nine chapters of the first edition, as the topics have continued to be relevant. The analysis of the effects of the first oil shock can readily be applied to the second.

The passage which seemed to create the greatest interest in the first edition was 'when is there a balance of payments problem?' (pp. 43–51). Here I have added a qualification, but have also pursued the issue of the desirability or otherwise of current-account imbalance further in Chapter 12.

Australian National University, Canberra
February 1985

PREFACE TO THE FIRST EDITION

THIS book originated in the William H. Abbott lectures which I gave at the Graduate School of Business of the University of Chicago in early 1976, and which also formed the basis of a lecture course the same year in Oxford. My greatest debt is to Robert Z. Aliber who arranged my visit to Chicago, extended warm hospitality, and talked to me at length about many aspects of the lectures as well as giving detailed comments on the manuscript. I am also indebted to William H. Abbott for financing my visit, to Dean Rosett and the Graduate School for their kind hospitality, and to Stephen Magee of the School for extensive comments. In thinking about the various issues I have been much influenced by lengthy discussions while striding along the banks of the Isis with my Oxford colleague Peter Oppenheimer, and his thoughtful comments at a later stage gave me many days' work of revising the manuscript. I am also indebted for comments to Anthony Bottrill, Carlos Diaz-Alejandro, John Flemming, Jacob Frenkel (Chapter 3), Harry Johnson (Chapters 10 and 11), John Martin, Theo Peeters (Chapters 10 and 11), and Frances Ruane. John Black helped improve my style. Finally, I am grateful to Penny Sylvester, who typed the manuscript with her usual speed, accuracy, and neatness.

Nuffield College, Oxford
September 1976

CONTENTS

INTRODUCTION

THIS book deals with five topics in international monetary economics. Much of the book was inspired by the economic events of the three dramatic years 1973, 1974, and 1975, especially the middle year, and by the new thinking that took hold in those years. While at the time the book was written the topics were of considerable current interest, the approach is essentially analytical. Theory is used for the analysis of practical problems and much emphasis is given to the appropriate construction of models. The last three chapters were written in 1985 and are concerned with the macro-economic interactions between major O.E.C.D. economies.

The five topics are balance of payments theories, old and new, inflation and exchange rates, the international adjustment to the oil-price rise, monetary integration in Europe, and the world of flexible exchange rates and capital mobility. A central issue running through the whole book is the role of exchange-rate variation as an instrument of economic policy.

Chapter 1 expounds the 'two-targets two-instruments' model of balance-of-payments policy where the distinction between traded and non-traded goods is crucial to the exposition. Internal and external balance are the two targets, and absorption and switching the two proximate instruments. This version of the model has become very popular, and is well known to specialists in the field. It is presented here as a foundation for later analysis.

Chapter 2 extends the previous model to allow for wage rigidity and income distribution effects. First it expounds the implications of holding money wages constant, rather than the money prices of non-traded goods. The effects of devaluation then depend on the production structure; for example, whether capital is mobile between the traded and non-traded sectors or whether one sector is labour-intensive relative to the other. Then it deals with the income distribution effects of devaluation, a matter that is often neglected. The effects of expenditure reduction on income distribution are taken into account, the point being that an expenditure (absorption) reduction is a crucial component of an improvement in the current account of the balance of payments. This income-distribution analysis is used for studying the effects of downward rigidity of *real* wages.

Chapter 3 is concerned with the 'monetary theory of the balance of payments'. Some of the main points that are stressed in this approach are expounded and incorporated here into the basic model of the first chapter. The aim is to show the relationship between different theories. This chapter takes note of some of the insights of the monetary theory and questions what seems to be its central emphasis on the demand and supply of money. Furthermore, the effects of both monetary and of fiscal policy on international capital movements are introduced, the exchange rate being fixed. In analysing the effects of a monetary expansion, use is made of a portfolio balance model. At the end, the question is asked: What is a balance-of-payments problem? This is an important, though neglected question, and, admittedly, it is not fully answered here, though a somewhat radical suggestion, throwing doubt on the importance of the balance of payments as such, is put forward.

Chapter 4 presents a systematic model for thinking about the effects of the exchange-rate regime on inflation. Is a fixed- or a flexible-rate regime more inflationary? The approach focuses on the policy choices of monetary authorities rather than on automatic monetary processes. In this respect it differs from the approaches widely current in the literature. The point is that the rate of inflation depends on what the monetary authorities choose to do, and the issue is how their choices will be influenced by the exchange-rate regime. The general conclusion is that the introduction of more exchange-rate flexibility will make some countries more inflationary and some less, essentially allowing countries to choose their own inflation rates instead of having to bring their inflation rates close to the world inflation rate, as they have to do in a fixed-rate system.

Chapter 5 examines possible asymmetries which might cause the world rate of inflation to be higher or lower under one regime than the other. Two 'asymmetry' theories that have been put forward are looked at sceptically. This chapter can be regarded as qualifying the conclusions of the previous chapter, but does not in fact yield the conclusion that either exchange-rate regime has clearly a more inflationary bias.

Chapter 6 asks: Is the United States a source of world inflation? Did its reserve currency role encourage it to be inflationary? Need

other countries have 'imported' inflation? The issues discussed here
have been a great source of controversy. This chapter tries to treat
them more systematically than is usual, and to relate the discussion
to the basic model of Chapter 4.

Chapter 7 presents a theoretical framework for analysing the
short-run macro-economic effects of the oil-price rise. The approach
has been implicit in much writing on the subject, but it seems useful
for students to have the model presented explicitly, with all
assumptions fully brought out.

Chapter 8 carries the model further to allow for balance-of-
payments effects among non-OPEC countries and to explain the role
of exchange rates. At the end there are some generalizations as to
what actually governed exchange-rate alterations and current
accounts in the two crucial years 1974–5. The tendency for real
exchange rates to stay constant over the period 1973–5 as a whole is
noted, and the four sources of current account imbalance are
distinguished.

Chapter 9 discusses the following three questions. First, why did
the world go into recession in 1974–5? The particular issue here is
the role of the oil-price rise in bringing about world recession.
Secondly, why did international liquidity increase, and what does it
mean? Here an attempt is made to explain how nominal world
reserves rose (though real reserves fell), and why little significance
could be attached to figures of 'official settlements balances' of
different countries, especially the United States. Finally, the
question is discussed: Was there need for international co-ordination
of policies and for current-account targets, as was widely thought in
1974? The general answer is that there appears not to have been any
great need for these.

Chapter 10 looks briefly at the European monetary-integration
issue. It asks whether the arguments for and against have been
affected by the great inflation of 1972–3 and by the new views about
the limited ability of monetary policy to affect employment. It also
describes the European Monetary System and assesses its record so
far. Is it a significant move towards monetary integration?

Chapter 11 deals with the way in which the effects of monetary-
and fiscal-policy changes in one large country are transmitted to
other countries when exchange rates are flexible and capital is
mobile. The presentation is in terms of a two-country model. A
distinction is made beween transmission through the terms of

trade—economic expansion in one country improving the terms of trade of the other and hence inducing expansion in the second country—a form of *positive transmission* which is called here the *locomotive effect*—and transmission through the capital market, which also affects the terms of trade but involves current-account imbalance. The possibility of *negative transmission* is also allowed for. The reactions both of wages and of monetary and fiscal policies in the second country are crucial in determining the final effects. The discussion is relevant to the analysis of a number of recent international policy issues, notably the debate about the *locomotive theory* and relative economic expansion of major O.E.C.D. countries that took place around 1978, and the effects of the U.S. budget deficit.

Chapter 12 takes a very broad look at the international macro-economic system that has emerged unplanned out of the breakdown of Bretton Woods, the great inflation, and the oil shock. It is a *laissez-faire* system, where governments are major actors and follow whatever policies, including exchange rate policies, they choose. An important feature, of course, is that real exchange rates between major O.E.C.D. economies have varied greatly, and that capital is highly mobile. Does the system have a logic, and to what exent is it efficient or optimal? The question of the desirability of current-account imbalances and real exchange-rate changes associated in particular with Japan and the United States is discussed.

Chapter 13 deals with the much-debated question of policy co-ordination. What are possible forms of co-ordination (always between the major O.E.C.D. economies), and are they desirable? In what direction should countries try to influence each others' policies? Is policy synchronization—which may be able to avoid large changes in real exchange rates—desirable?

Many of the chapters in this book were inspired by an attempt to understand the events of 1974, and to a lesser extent 1975, but if this book makes any contribution at all it should be with its methods of analysis or the framework of theory presented rather than in judgements or assessments of the events of a particular year. This also applies to the last three chapters, which refer to debates about the Japanese surpluses of 1977 and 1978, to the great recession of 1980–2, and, above all, to the U.S. fiscal and current-account deficits, which became major issues around the time these chapters were written.

BALANCE OF PAYMENTS THEORY:
OLD AND NEW

I

A MODEL OF
BALANCE OF PAYMENTS POLICY

THE aim in this and the next two chapters is to take a good look at the basic model for analysing balance-of-payments policy that many of us have been using for some years. In this chapter I shall expound it, and then in the next two chapters I shall introduce various complications and mention difficulties and issues that go beyond the model.

Initially I am going to over-simplify the basic model in order to focus on the main points. Criticisms will be constructive since the basic model probably needs to be adapted, or incorporated in a more general model, rather than to be thrown away. The model will be for a single country; it is not a *world* model. Therefore one should not think of using it directly for a very large country— i.e. the United States, Germany, or Japan—where various international repercussions cannot be neglected.

In the first two chapters I shall ignore monetary considerations, capital movements, and portfolio-balance objectives, all matters that have recently been much emphasized by Chicago-based or trained economists but have been ignored or underplayed in what I call the 'basic model'. I shall come to these matters in the third chapter.

Absorption and Switching[1]

Let us suppose to start with that the country concerned is running a deficit in the current account of its balance of payments. We ignore private capital movements, whether short-term or long-term, and in fact assume them away. Hence the country is running down its foreign-exchange reserves. Alternatively its government or central bank might borrow abroad to finance the

[1] Appendix I (p. 19 below) represents geometrically the main arguments of this passage.

deficit, but it will be simplest to suppose that the reserves decline. This situation of current-account deficit in the absence of any private capital inflow is generally described as a situation of *external imbalance*.

At the same time, let us suppose that there is *internal balance*. This is usually interpreted as meaning that demand for domestic goods and services is sufficient to ensure their full employment at a constant price-level. But since the term 'full employment' is an ambiguous and really not very meaningful concept it is best taken to mean that increased output of some industries can only be brought about by reducing the resources available to some other industries, and that this resource shift requires some change in relative prices.

An important tool of analysis is the conceptual division of industries into those producing *tradables* and those producing *non-tradables*. Tradables consist of *exportables* and *importables*. Exportables, in turn, consist of actual exports as well as of close substitutes for exports that are sold domestically, like beef sold to Argentinians. Importables consist of imports as well as of goods produced domestically and sold domestically that are close substitutes for imports, i.e. import-competing goods. These tradables have their domestic prices determined broadly by the world market, subject only to tariffs, export subsidies, international transport costs, and, of course, the exchange rate. Finally, non-tradables consist of all those goods and services the prices of which are determined by supply and demand domestically. This category generally consists mainly of services.

Strictly it is only valid to aggregate exportables and importables into a composite commodity—tradables—if their relative prices do not change. But this presents no problem here. I shall be assuming such a constant price ratio between exportables and importables until later in this chapter, and again in the next chapter. Thus the terms of trade facing the country are assumed to be unaffected by its various policies. This is the 'small-country assumption'.

To return to the main argument, the domestic excess supply of exportables is equal to actual exports, while the domestic excess demand for importables is actual imports. Combining these two, there is thus balance-of-payments equilibrium if domestic excess demand for tradables is zero, and there is a deficit if the net excess demand is positive. Thus we start in our present story with domestic excess demand for tradables. By balance-of-payments deficit we mean, of course, a current-account deficit, and so, for this purpose, exportables and importables must be defined as including both visibles and invisibles.

At the same time I am assuming that there is initially equilibrium in the market for non-tradables, this being the situation of internal balance. Demand for non-tradables equals supply. Therefore, combining tradables and non-tradables, there is aggregate excess demand. Demand is generated by expenditure on consumption and investment, private and public. This is *absorption*: the economy *absorbs* goods and services for these various purposes. This absorption exceeds the national output or supply. Income is derived from output. Hence absorption exceeds income, and because it does so there is a balance-of-payments deficit.

The argument then goes on something like the following. There is external imbalance: so the foreign-exchange reserves are going down. Hence there is a problem. Something must be done about it. One obvious remedy would seem to be to reduce absorption by some kind of tightening in monetary or fiscal policy. Domestic demand for importables will then fall, and this will reduce imports; in addition, domestic demand for exportables will fall, and this will make more goods available for exports and so, to some extent, may increase exports. Excess demand for tradables can therefore certainly be eliminated if the cut in absorption is sufficient. But a reduction in absorption will also reduce demand for non-tradables. This is an unfortunate but inevitable by-product of this policy.

At this point a crucial, and quite realistic, assumption is introduced. The prices of non-tradables are rigid downwards. Reduced demand will lead then, not to price cuts, but to excess supply, inventory accumulation, and eventually unemployment. It must be remembered that relative prices have not changed, so that there is no inducement for resources to move out of non-tradables into the tradable-goods industries. Unemployment is thus inevitable if there was originally internal balance. External balance has been attained at the cost of losing internal balance.

The next step is to point out that if it is desired to attain two targets—external balance and internal balance—it is necessary to have *two* instruments. The absorption instrument is not enough. On its own it could not maintain full employment. The second

instrument required is a *switching* policy. This is a policy that
raises the domestic price of tradables relative to the price of non-
tradables and so causes patterns of production and of absorption to
switch. On the production side resources will be induced to move
out of production of non-traded goods into the production of
exportables and importables. This will reduce the excess supply of
non-tradables, and so help to restore internal balance, and at the
same time it will increase the supply of tradables, hence reducing
excess demand there, and helping to improve the balance-of-
payments. On the demand side the rise in the relative price of
tradables will shift the pattern of absorption away from tradables
and towards non-tradables, hence also reducing excess demand for
tradables and excess supply of non-tradables.

The switching policy can therefore offset the effects of the
absorption-reduction policy in the market for non-tradables. The
reduction in the absorption created excess supply of non-tradables
while the switching eliminated it. Both the reduction in absorption
and the switching policy reduced excess demand for tradables, and
thus both improved the balance of payments. It follows that when
the reduction in absorption is associated with the right switching
policy, the cut in absorption need not be as great as when the
whole balance-of-payments improvement has to be brought about
by an absorption reduction on its own. Finally, demand for
tradables will be equal to supply of them, and similarly in the case
of non-tradables. Thus for the economy as a whole, absorption
(expenditure) must eventually be equal to output (and hence
income).

We have seen that an absorption policy on its own would not be
satisfactory because it would create excess supply of non-traded
goods, and hence unemployment. Similarly, a switching policy on
its own would be no good. It could not succeed in improving the
balance-of-payments. To show this, let us imagine the relative
price of tradables to go up as a consequence of a pure switching
policy. In the first instance we can suppose demand for tradables
to be reduced and supply to be increased, so improving the balance
of payments. But this is not the end of the story.

The market for non-tradables will be adversely affected. At
constant absolute prices of non-tradables there will be excess demand for non-tradables as demand is switched towards them,
while at the same time resources have been induced to move out of

non-tradable production. Thus the prices of non-tradables will rise until excess demand for them has been eliminated. The reasonable assumption here is that the prices of non-tradables are flexible upwards, even though they are inflexible downwards. This price rise simply negates the initial switching policy. Finally, relative prices will have returned to where they started, and the original balance-of-payments improvement will have been reversed. If the prices of non-tradables were somewhat inflexible upwards—not a very realistic assumption—there might in the first instance be some involuntary savings to match the excess demand, but eventually the excess demand would spill over on to tradables so, again, reversing the original balance-of-payments improvement.

Role of Devaluation

An alteration in the exchange rate is seen in this model as the major *switching* device. I am assuming that the country concerned is small, so that it faces given world prices for its imports and exports. Let us think of Argentina here. We suppose that the prices of the manufactured goods it buys and of the wheat and beef that it sells are constant in dollar terms, quite unaffected by Argentinian supply, demand, or pricing policy. When the peso is devalued, the peso prices—i.e. the domestic prices—of the tradable goods go up. There will be a uniform percentage rise in the prices of all exportables and importables, including prices of exportables sold at home and prices of import-competing goods.

If the prices of non-tradables stay constant, there will then be a rise in the relative price of tradables, this relative price change bringing about the desired switching. It was noted earlier that the prices of non-tradables are assumed to be rigid downwards. But they are not assumed to be rigid upwards, so a rise in their prices must be avoided if the switching effect of the devaluation is not to be negated. Hence there must be an appropriate reduction in absorption associated with the devaluation if the latter is to be effective as a balance-of-payments improving device.

The devaluation is seen in this approach as an exogenous or parametric policy device. One can imagine that there is a market for foreign exchange and that the central bank determines the price in this market by drawing on its foreign-exchange reserves. In spite of excess demand for foreign exchange (which is excess supply of the home currency, the peso) the price does not rise because the central bank is selling some of its foreign-exchange reserves. The bank then makes a policy decision to sell less in a given time period, which brings the price of foreign exchange up. The peso is thus devalued, and we study the effects of this devaluation on domestic production and absorption.

Devaluation has not only a relative price or switching effect. It may also have an effect on absorption. It may itself bring about some of the necessary disabsorption in our example. It is even conceivable that it brings about, by chance, all the disabsorption that is needed. Indeed, it may even overshoot the mark and produce too much disabsorption. This aspect becomes important in the monetary approach, so I only deal with it briefly at this stage.

The simple point can be made as follows. Suppose that fiscal and monetary policy kept the level of *money* expenditure constant. The devaluation would then have reduced *real* expenditure because it has raised the average domestic price-level. (The prices of traded goods have risen while the prices of non-traded goods have remained unchanged.) Thus absorption in real terms will have fallen. Just looking at the demand side, the rise in the price of tradables, with total money expenditure constant, will lead to a rise in demand for non-tradables on account of a switching (substitution) effect and a fall on account of a disabsorption (income) effect.

Without pursuing this further now, the main point to note is that the appropriate disabsorption policy—i.e. fiscal or monetary policy, or both—must take into account whatever automatic disabsorption has already been brought about by the devaluation. This is a consideration which has tended to be underplayed in this approach. We have supposed that the appropriate disabsorption policy will take place, and have stressed the problems that arise if there is a failure to disabsorb sufficiently—or if there is too much disabsorption—but we have not focused on the details of the disabsorption policy and how much is brought about automatically by devaluation.

Usefulness of the Basic Model

This basic model is undoubtedly very useful, and focuses on important matters that are not always clearly understood. It brings out a particular role for the exchange rate. Without disabsorption the balance of payments cannot improve, and—in the case considered—a devaluation cannot improve the balance of payments, except perhaps temporarily and except in so far as it is allowed to have a disabsorption effect. But a devaluation conceived of as a switching device is still necessary because it makes it possible to avoid unemployment while the disabsorption policy improves the balance of payments.

It is particularly important to bring out that, when one starts in internal balance, some disabsorption is necessary if the balance of payments is to improve. The disabsorption represents a cut in real spending and thus, in a sense, is a sacrifice. To the extent that the devaluation itself brings about some disabsorption, it produces some of the sacrifice. A relative price change on its own—pure switching—may seem like a soft option, a gimmick that improves the balance of payments and yet avoids real expenditure cuts. But this is shown to be wrong. If there is no disabsorption there will be no improvement.

Recently there has been much discussion in Britain about the use of import quotas. Their effects would be rather similar to a devaluation. A system of import quotas, like a devaluation, is a switching device. In the British situation, which is not unlike the one described in our example here, both disabsorption and switching are likely to be needed. But it has not always been realized that without the appropriate disabsorption—a politically painful process—import quotas are unlikely to have any beneficial effects on the balance-of-payments, other than, perhaps, in the very short run. This, of course, leaves aside the large issue of the choice between quotas and devaluation.

The model is certainly an improvement on the way these matters were approached in earlier years.

A popular technique has been the elasticities approach. The effects of a devaluation are studied in terms of demand and supply curves for imports and exports, these in turn being derived from demand and supply curves for importables and exportables. A great deal of interest has come out of this approach, and it ought not to be dismissed completely. Essentially it focuses on relative-price or switching effects, while pushing absorption effects into the background. In terms of the present model, one can best make sense of the elasticities approach by interpreting it as making the implicit assumption that absorption is always automatically varied so as to maintain equilibrium in the market for non-traded goods at a constant price-level for these goods. But the need for an appropriate absorption policy was certainly not stressed.

One version of the elasticities approach rested on a different, more Keynesian basis. It assumed that there was Keynesian unemployment of labour and other factors of production in the non-traded sector, and that this prevented the prices of non-tradables from rising. A devaluation would then have a multiplier effect which would increase domestic demand for tradables that would have to be subtracted from the initial favourable switching effect on the balance of payments.

The essential improvement of the approach presented here is the focus on *two* instruments and *two* targets, and not just one. The elasticities approach in its non-Keynesian version swept this problem under the carpet by assuming that one instrument—absorption policy—always attained one target—internal balance. At the same time it must be noted that the so-called instruments—absorption and switching—are really only proximate; the ultimate instruments are the exchange rate, tax scales and so on, and these could have *both* absorption and switching effects.

Another way in which this model improves on earlier models is in distinguishing between tradables and non-tradables. The important switching effect of a devaluation comes about because the price ratio between these two categories of goods is being altered. The terms of trade—that is, the price ratio between exportables and importables—do not need to alter. In earlier models a devaluation usually worsened the terms of trade. This is certainly a possibility, as we shall see below, but it is not inevitable.

Some Simple Extensions of the Basic Model

It is obvious that the whole approach could be applied to a country which is running a surplus and so accumulating foreign exchange. In that case external balance calls for an increase in absorption, since switching alone would lead to unemployment. One would expect an increase in absorption to be politically attractive. It could be brought about, for example, by a rise in public spending. So the reluctance of Germany at various times in recent years to make adjustments sufficient to eliminate her large balance-of-payments surplus is surprising. But we shall come later to a possible reason for this reluctance which is not clearly brought out in the present approach.

One can also extend the analysis to a two-country or a multi-country one. This is fairly simple. Suppose we have a two-country world. Each country produces its own non-traded goods, and in addition there are two traded goods, the importable of one country being the exportable of the other. One country's deficit is then the other country's surplus. If we have a numeraire, such as gold or SDRs, we can express each exchange rate in terms of this numeraire. Equilibrium can then be established by either the surplus country appreciating or the deficit country depreciating, or some combination of the two. But, if internal balance is to be maintained, this must be accompanied by an appropriate increase in absorption in the surplus country and decrease in absorption in the deficit country. If the deficit country successfully resists a reduction in absorption it will not be possible to restore international-payments equilibrium. On the other hand, if the surplus country resists an increase in absorption it will still be possible to attain balance-of-payments equilibrium, but only at the cost of unemployment in the surplus country.

One might balk at the concept of an 'importable' good used in this type of model. This implies that import-competing goods are perfect substitutes for imports, so that the domestic prices of import-competing goods are fully determined by the domestic prices of imports. Because of product differentiation there is rarely such close substitutability. While it is a matter of degree, in principle one could assume that there is no domestic production of import-ables at all—that all are actually imported—and then one could include all import-competing goods in the non-tradable sector. This would change nothing in the basic analysis.

Finally, one could make a distinction between fiscal and monetary policy, and indeed between different forms of either type of policy. A given reduction in absorption can be obtained with various combinations of these policies—some increases in personal-income-tax, some increases in corporate-tax, some decreases in government spending, some credit contraction to the housing sector, and so on. But changing the mix of these policies may have a *switching* effect. For example, if the non-tradable content in housing expenditures is greater than in spending out of corporate profits, a shift in the pattern of an absorption reduction which involves higher corporate-tax but makes relatively more finance available for housing will have a switching effect similar to a devaluation: it will switch expenditures away from tradables towards non-tradables.

Thus one really needs to know the composition of absorption policy in order to determine how much deliberate switching (exchange-rate) policy is needed. This parallels the earlier point that the absorption content in the switching policy of devaluation affects the extent to which further deliberate disabsorption is needed. The model is deprived of some of its simplicity when one realizes that very few policies do not have both an absorption and a switching content.

Terms of Trade Effects Introduced

Any possible changes in the terms of trade have been ignored so far. The effects of absorption changes and of devaluation on the terms of trade clearly need to be taken into account. The simplicity of the basic model hinges on the assumption that the country concerned is genuinely small, so that it cannot affect its terms of trade. The terms of trade can certainly be allowed to alter for exogenous reasons, but the quantity of its imports the country buys must not affect its import prices and the quantity of its exports that it unloads on world markets similarly must not affect their prices. With this assumption a devaluation has the same proportionate effect on the domestic prices of exports as of imports. Furthermore, it becomes justifiable to treat exportables and importables as if they were part of one composite commodity—the tradable—since there is no relative price change within the composite.

If one wants to allow for terms of trade effects one should, at the minimum, have a three-good model—exportables, importables, and non-tradables—for the single country. The main ideas can be explained if one superimposes on the basic model a foreign-price effect on the export side. We continue to assume that the country cannot affect its import prices in foreign-currency terms. But now, the more it exports, the more the foreign-currency prices of exports fall. Since the foreign-currency prices of imports are constant, export prices can be measured in terms of imports.

Both the reduction in absorption and the switching policy will increase the quantity of exports for the reasons that follow from the basic model. This increased export quantity will then cause export prices to fall. In addition it will modify the original increase in exports because the fall in the foreign prices of exports will cause their domestic prices to fall somewhat relative to the situation before this terms-of-trade effect. Since the increases in the domestic prices of exportables induced the switching between exportables and non-tradables in the first place, the net result will be a lesser rise in the quantity of exports. But some rise in the export quantity will remain, at least provided production and demand patterns respond to relative price changes.

The crucial question remains whether the rise in the quantity of exports will lead to a rise in their foreign-currency value. If it leads to a fall in value—that is, if the foreign elasticity of demand is less than unity—then the analysis has to be modified in a significant way. On the other hand, if the elasticity is unity or more, there is no problem at all. All the preceding discussion stands (although, of course, the 'numbers' will be different in any particular case). It remains true that both a reduction in absorption and a devaluation will increase the quantity and value of exports. Even when the value of exports falls while the quantity rises, the main argument could still stand. A reduction in absorption might still improve the balance of payments, because the improvement on the side of imports might outweigh the worsening on the side of exports; and similarly in the case of a devaluation. Of course, the terms-of-trade effect represents a real loss to the country; therefore, the reduction in real absorption that has to go with a given balance of payments improvement has to be larger than in the absence of such an adverse terms-of-trade effect, as also has the devaluation required.

Here it should also be noted that the foreign-currency value of exports might fall in the short run as the result of a devaluation even when there is no increase in the quantity of exports at all. The *domestic*-currency price might be rigid in a short period, perhaps because of contracts or administered pricing, so that the *foreign*-currency price falls. This leads to the so-called J-curve effect: at first the foreign-currency value of exports falls, and then later, as domestic prices respond, it rises. The domestic price could have been increased immediately after the devaluation without sales being lost as a result, but it was not. Alternatively, it might be increased somewhat, but not as much as is possible on a short-run market basis. The foreign-currency price will then fall when the country devalues, and if the quantity does not increase much, the value of exports will fall, just as in the case where the foreign elasticity of demand was less than unity.

The terms-of-trade effect just discussed can be important. But I shall ignore it in the next two chapters in order to focus on other matters. Thus I shall return to the so-called 'small-country assumption' where the country concerned faces given import supply and export demand prices abroad. But this does not mean that the discussion to follow is not relevant for large countries; it means only that for such countries something should really be added about terms of trade effects—and this would have to be done even for those countries that are not really large but are nevertheless significant world suppliers of some of their exports.

APPENDIX

ABSORPTION AND SWITCHING FOR INTERNAL AND EXTERNAL BALANCE

In Figure 1 tradables are shown on the vertical axis and non-tradables on the horizontal axis. TT′ is the full employment transformation curve. Initially production is at the point B, determined by the slope of the line G′G, which indicates the initial price ratio. Income measured in non-tradables is OG. Initial expenditure measured in terms of non-tradables is OH and the initial absorption point is D. Thus expenditure exceeds income by GH. The indifference curve tangential to H′H at D represents a constant level of *real* absorption. Demand and supply for non-tradables are equal. But demand for tradables exceeds their supply by BD, this being the initial balance-of-payments deficit.

If expenditure is reduced but the price ratio is kept unchanged, the absorption point will move down OZ towards O, the curve OZ being a sort of Engel curve. If expenditure were reduced to OG it would be equal to full employment income. But there would be a residual balance-of-payments deficit and excess supply of non-tradables. If expenditure were reduced further, to OF, there would be balance-of-payments equilibrium, but excess supply of non-tradables of EB. The latter would lead to reduced production of non-tradables, and hence unemployment, and finally the production point would be at E.

There is internal and external balance at A, where an indifference curve is tangential to the transformation curve. JJ′ is tangential to the transformation curve at A, and its slope indicates the price ratio appropriate to internal and external balance. A switching policy could establish this price ratio, bringing the absorption pattern to some point on the curve OZ′, while the appropriate absorption policy could bring the absorption point to A.

A pure switching policy—one that kept real absorption constant but raised the domestic price of tradables—would bring the absorption point to K, which is on the same indifference curve as the initial point D. This would yield excess demand for non-tradables of K′K, which would raise their price, and so negate the original switching, returning absorption to D.

One can imagine the restoration of external balance, while maintaining internal balance, to be reached in various ways. First

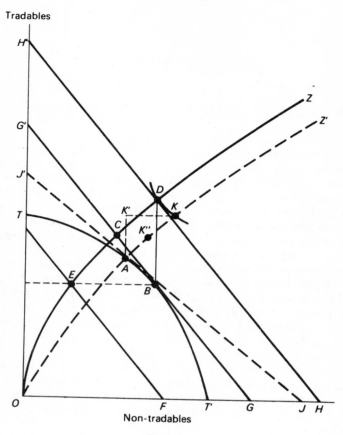

FIG. 1

there might be a switching policy, possibly incorporating some dis-absorption in real terms, bringing the economy to some point on OZ' below K, such as K''. This could be a devaluation. Then expenditure would be reduced by fiscal or monetary policy to OJ (measured in non-tradables) bringing the absorption point to A. Alternatively, first ex-penditure might be reduced to the level of full employment income, bringing the absorption point to C, and then switching brings it to A. In this case switching will involve a fall in real absorption (since the indifference curve through A is below that through C) but a rise in money expenditure (with given money price of non-tradables), the expenditure increase (again, in terms of non-tradables) being GJ.

REFERENCES

The 'two-targets two-instruments' approach to balance-of-payments theory originated in J. E. Meade, *The Balance of Payments*, Oxford University Press, London, 1951. Also a lanamark in this field, which introduced the concept of switching, is H. G. Johnson, 'Towards a General Theory of the Balance of Payments', in H. G. Johnson, *International Trade and Economic Growth*, Allen & Unwin, London, 1958. The geometric small-country model with traded and non-traded goods, which forms the basis of the approach in this chapter, was first presented in W. E. G. Salter, 'Internal and External Balance: The Role of Price and Expenditure Effects', *Economic Record*, 35 (August 1959), 226–38. A basic reference on the elasticities analysis of devaluation is G. Haberler, 'The Market for Foreign Exchange and the Stability of the Balance of Payments: A Theoretical Analysis', *Kyklos*, 3 (1949), 193–218. The elasticities approach is integrated with this Salter model in R. Dornbusch, 'Exchange Rates and Fiscal Policy in a Popular Model of International Trade', *American Economic Review*, 65 (December 1975), 859–71.

2

WAGE RIGIDITY, INCOME DISTRIBUTION, AND BALANCE-OF-PAYMENTS POLICY

A CRUCIAL assumption of the model expounded in the previous chapter has been that the prices of non-tradables are rigid downwards. This has meant that a reduction in demand for non-tradables as a result of a reduction in total absorption has led to excess supply and hence unemployment, rather than to a fall in their money prices. Hence a switching policy has been necessary to maintain full employment. Furthermore, we have supposed that the combination of absorption and switching policies has prevented the prices of non-traded goods from rising. It follows that the rise in the domestic prices of tradables resulting from a devaluation has led to a rise to the same extent in their prices *relative* to non-tradables. It is this relative-price effect that has led to switching of the production and demand patterns.

In this chapter I shall look at three alternative assumptions. First, one might assume that commodity and factor prices are flexible downwards. Secondly, one might assume that money wages, and not money prices of non-tradable commodities, are rigid downwards, and in addition are prevented from rising by the combination of the two policies. And thirdly, one might assume some *real* rather than money rigidity, and in particular, downward rigidity of *real* wages. The last assumption would be the most radical. Before examining it in detail it will be necessary to look at the income-distribution effects of restoring external balance and of devaluation.

Factor-Price Flexibility

If commodity and factor prices were flexible downwards there would be no need for a switching *policy*. Starting in balance-of-payments deficit and full employment, absorption would be reduced in order to eliminate the deficit. In the first instance this might yield excess supply of non-tradables. So their prices would fall. This price fall would bring about the same rise in the prices of tradables relative to non-tradables as the devaluation would have done. The only difference in the final outcome is that this time the average price-level—of tradables and non-tradables combined—falls, instead of rising.

The main point is that there is now *automatic* switching. The prices of non-tradables will fall until full employment in the non-tradable sector has been restored; this is brought about by a movement of resources out of this sector into tradables, induced by the price fall, and by a shift of demand towards it, also induced by the price fall. There is thus no need for an instrument designed to maintain internal balance, since price flexibility automatically maintains internal balance. The instrument would only be needed if the maintenance of price stability—in the present case, prevention of price declines—were an objective of policy.

Downward Rigidity of Money Wages

The second alternative assumption is to let money wages be rigid downwards, rather than the money prices of non-tradables. This assumption would be more in conformity with the usual Keynesian models, and does seem more realistic. It does not actually make a great deal of difference to the model. But let us see in detail what it means. I shall consider three possible models.

One possibility is that there is a constant percentage profit margin in the non-tradable sector, 'cost-plus' pricing being the rule in that sector. This is the *cost-plus* model. In that case rigidity of the money wage would also mean rigidity of the prices of non-tradables. This is probably the most sensible interpretation of the rigid commodity-price assumption of the basic model. A devaluation then raises the profit margin in the tradable sector while the margin in the non-tradable sector stays unchanged.

A second possibility is that there is, at least in the short run, immobility of capital between the two sectors, but that profit rates are not rigid. I shall call this the *capital immobility model*. When a switching policy raises the demand for resources in the tradable sector, profits rise in that sector. With money wages constant, the absolute-profit rise per unit of output is equal to the rise in the domestic price resulting from devaluation. At the same time, labour will be drawn out of non-tradables into tradables and this will cause the profit margin to fall in the non-tradable sector. The assumption is that full employment of capital is maintained by profit flexibility. Capital will have less labour to work with in that sector, and so will be less profitable. Hence, with money wages constant, the money price of non-tradables will finally fall. To sum up, we hold money wages constant, and let profits in tradables go up and profits in non-tradables go down. We end up with the relative prices of tradables having risen not only because their money prices have risen owing to the devaluation but also because the money prices of non-tradables have fallen. The switching effect of a devaluation is therefore strengthened. The size of the devaluation required is then less than if the price of non-tradables had been rigid downwards.

A third possibility is that all factors are mobile and factor-intensities differ between industries. Hence we introduce elements of the standard *neo-classical trade model*. Let us suppose that we have two sectors, tradables and non-tradables, and two factors of production, labour and capital. Both factors are mobile between the two sectors, by contrast with the previous cases, where capital was immobile. Hence factor prices facing the two sectors are always the same. One sector is labour-intensive and the other is capital-intensive. Bearing in mind that non-tradables consist to a great extent of services, the realistic assumption is that non-tradables are relatively labour-intensive: the ratio of labour to capital employed in the non-tradable sector is higher than that in the tradable sector.

In that case, with non-tradables labour-intensive, we get the following result. Money wages are held constant, absorption being so adjusted as to maintain the total demand for labour equal to the supply at the original money wage. The domestic price of tradables has been raised by the devaluation. With money wages given this must mean a rise in the profit rate there. This rise in profits in the tradable sector attracts capital out of non-tradables, and thus forces profits up in that sector. Hence the prices of non-tradables must also rise. While the rate of profit per unit of capital must finally rise to the same extent in both sectors, profits (or 'the rental on capital goods') are a smaller part of costs in the non-tradable than in the tradable sector because the former is the labour-intensive sector. Hence the prices of non-tradables rise by less than the prices of tradables.

The conclusion in this case is that the devaluation causes the prices of both tradables *and* non-tradables to increase, but—because non-tradables are labour-intensive—the prices of the latter rise to a lesser extent. There will thus still be a switching effect resulting from a devaluation, but it will be somewhat modified because there is *some* rise in the prices of non-tradables, even though a smaller one than in the price of tradables.

In all three models the qualitative results of the basic model are not altered by the assumption that money wages, rather than the prices of non-tradable commodities, are rigid. The new assumption means only that the effect of a devaluation in raising the domestic prices of tradables relative to non-tradables, and hence bringing about switching, may be reinforced (in the capital-immobility model) or modified (in the neo-classical trade model with non-tradables labour-intensive); but it will not be negated.

Which Assumption is Best?

What is the best assumption to make—price flexibility, money-wage rigidity, or, perhaps, some kind of real-wage rigidity? No one would suggest that money prices are instantaneously flexible downwards. Until recently few people would have seriously considered a model where money wages were flexible downwards: the influence of Keynesian theories as well as common sense was too strong. But now we have the monetary models of the balance of payments which do seem to make that assumption. I have doubts about the assumption, but nevertheless, some argument for it can be made along the following lines.

It can be argued that all this analysis must be superimposed on a situation of general inflation. We imagine all prices to be rising continuously. Relative price changes are then brought about by some prices rising faster than others. The assumption that excess supply for labour will not cause money wages to fall—the assumption of money-wage rigidity downwards—must then be restated as the assumption that the continuous rise in the level of money-wages will not be affected by excess supply of labour. An assumption of downward flexibility of money-wages can then be reinterpreted as meaning that excess supply of labour will soon lead to a slackening of the rate of money-wage increase until the excess supply has been eliminated. It may never be necessary for money-wages to fall absolutely.

Perhaps the right approach is to suppose that in the short run there is some, if not absolute, downward rigidity, even in the rate of increase in wages, but in time flexibility emerges. The basic model, with its fundamental Keynesian assumption, is then a short-run model, and the issue then simply becomes how short the short run is, whether indeed it has been becoming shorter in recent years, and to what extent policy should be concerned with the short run.

Income Distribution: Effects of Switching

The income-distribution effects of restoring external balance and of a devaluation have so far been ignored. It is true that they are implicit in the reference to money-wages and profits, but it is time to make *real*-income effects explicit. Without taking these into account it is difficult to explain varying attitudes to balance-of-payments policies in different countries and in different sectors of the community. Similarly, one cannot understand why some policies failed when they ought to have succeeded on the basis of our simple model.

Let us begin by assuming money-wage rigidity, and suppose that a combination of disabsorption and switching by means of fiscal or monetary policies and devaluation has restored external balance while maintaining internal balance. Thus, to begin with, I assume success in these policies, although I shall reconsider this assumption later. I want to compare the real incomes of different sectors of the community before these policies operated and afterwards. In particular, I want to ask whether it is inevitable that real wages have to fall, since it is often said that a devaluation must lower real wages if it is to improve the balance of payments.

One has to remember now that initially expenditure exceeded income, this excess being the balance of payments deficit. The restoration of external balance has two aspects. Firstly, expenditure has to be brought down to the level of income. Secondly, there is a relative commodity-price change which is designed to induce switching. I shall begin with this second aspect and consider the income-distribution effects of this switching mechanism. Here our earlier analysis becomes very relevant. The domestic price of tradables relative to that of non-tradables has risen. What happens to real wages and profits because of this? Let us look at this in terms of the two models we used earlier.

In the *capital-immobility model* labour was mobile between the two sectors, but capital was specific to each sector. It will be recalled that, with the money-wage constant, a devaluation caused profits to rise in the tradable sector and to fall in the non-tradable sector. The money price of tradables rose and of non-tradables fell. In that case it is quite clear that real profits rose in the tradable sector and fell in the non-tradable sector, changing in the same direction, but to a lesser extent, than money profits. Thus there is a very significant inter-sectoral income-redistribution effect. But real wages could rise or fall. Money-wages are constant, domestic prices of tradables have risen because of the devaluation and prices of non-tradables have fallen. It is thus even conceivable that real wages rise.

It is an interesting and somewhat surprising result that a devaluation could cause real wages to rise. Usually one assumes that real wages must fall because the prices of tradables are raised by the devaluation. But this neglects the point that demand for non-tradables falls, causing profits there to be squeezed and their prices to fall. Yet one should not make too much of this possibility, since non-tradables tend to have a relatively low profit content.

Perhaps it would be better to use the *neo-classical trade model*, where both labour and capital are mobile between the two industries and there is a uniform rate of profit in the economy as a whole. With non-tradables assumed to be labour-intensive, and their relative price having fallen as a result of devaluation, there must then be a fall in the real wage. This is easily seen if we recall that the money-wage is constant, the price of tradables rises by the amount of the devaluation and the prices of non-tradables also rise, though to a lesser extent. The counterpart of this result is that real profits must rise, since the relative price of the capital-intensive product has gone up.

One could generalize this approach as follows. Consider a country with many industries, all with different factor-intensities. In addition, there are many factors of production. The switching policy brings about a set of relative-price changes, in general raising prices of exportables and goods that are close substitutes for imports, and lowering relative prices of goods that are only distantly substitutable. Factors specific to or intensive in the tradable industries will tend to have their real incomes raised; and the reverse for factors specific to or intensive in the non-tradable sectors. It is a general equilibrium problem. Some people gain, some lose. But there is no general theoretical reason why wage-earners as a whole should lose, unless one inserts—no doubt realistically—an assumption that the whole category of non-tradables is relatively labour-intensive.

One should also add that switching has income-distribution effects because of demand differences. When the prices of tradables rise relative to those of non-tradables, then those people who are heavy consumers of tradables are likely to lose relative to those who have preferences for non-tradables. For example, if foods are primarily non-tradables, and the share of expenditure on food is higher for wage-earners than for others, a rise in the relative price of tradables would shift income distribution towards wage-earners on this account. In general this aspect of switching will be ignored here, but one can easily allow for it.

Income Distribution: Effects of Expenditure Reduction

Having looked at the effects of switching on income distribution we must now look at the other aspect of the balance-of-payments improvement: the reduction in aggregate expenditure or absorption. If the deficit is to be eliminated completely expenditure must be reduced to the level of income. It is then necessary to face up to the question of why expenditure exceeded income initially and how the excess of expenditure was financed. Here let us assume that there was a fiscal deficit financed by credit creation by the central bank, and that this is eliminated either by an increase in tax rates or a cut in public expenditure.

In order to introduce the real income effects of these fiscal changes into our analysis we must distinguish *earned* income, *disposable* income, *social* income, and *total* income, and similarly for the components of income—wages and profits. Earned income is the pre-tax income derived from production. Our analysis so far has only been concerned with earned income, and when we have referred to the real wage, it has been the earned real wage. Disposable income is earned income plus transfers minus taxes. Social income is the value of the services provided by government non-transfer expenditure, and total income is the sum of disposable and social income. Changes in the pattern of domestic output induced by switching policies affect, as we have seen, the pattern of earned income. Now we introduce the effects of tax increases and government expenditure reductions in order to determine what happens to *total* real income and to its components, total real wages and total real profits. To isolate these effects for the moment, we hold earned income and its components constant.

If the public expenditures that are reduced gave no one any satisfaction—being neither transfers nor a form of social income— then there are no effects on total real income. This is an extreme case. If social services are cut, both the social wage and the disposable wage are likely to be reduced, so that the total wage falls on both counts. Some of the government revenue may have been used, as in Britain at present, to subsidize food and so keep down the cost of living to the wage-earner, in which case cutting this expenditure will reduce the real total wage. Perhaps business loses out in government services, or through failure of public infra-structure being maintained, so that the real value of total profits falls. If public investment has been cut, then real total incomes of those members of the community that could expect to benefit from these in the future have fallen. On balance it is certainly likely that the expenditure reductions would lead to some cut in real total wages. When the fiscal deficit is reduced by an increase in taxation, such a real total wage cut is even more likely.

One should also take into account the interest payments to be received in the future by the central bank on those of its foreign-exchange reserves which it is able to retain because of the elimination of the deficit. The expectation of these interest payments represents a rise in real incomes for taxpayers, who include wage-earners. This effect is usually neglected. In principle it could outweigh all the other effects, but is unlikely to do so if wage-earners heavily discount future expected incomes.

Income Distribution: Switching and Expenditure Reduction Combined

To the income-distribution effects of switching one must thus add the real income effects of the expenditure reduction. It is likely that the real total wage will fall on both counts: the earned real wage will fall as a result of switching (at least in the neo-classical model with non-tradables labour-intensive); and the disposable real wage will fall even more because of tax increases and reduced transfers, while the social wage will fall because of reduced expenditures. By contrast, the real income of capital before tax and before taking into account reduced benefits from government expenditures might indeed rise as a result of switching—and must do so in the model where non-tradables are labour-intensive—but it might nevertheless fall once the adverse tax and government expenditure effects are added in. In other words, *earned* profits may rise and yet *total* profits may fall.

When one takes these income distribution effects into account it is not difficult to see why countries are often reluctant to make significant discrete alterations in their exchange rates, whether to devalue or to revalue. The expenditure reduction that needs to go with the devaluation is likely to have adverse effects on various sections of the community, including wage-earners—at least if prospective benefits from future interest earnings on foreign reserves are ignored or not rated highly. In addition, there may be a redistribution against some sectors. In the case of the devaluation a fall in real wages on this account seems rather likely.

It is interesting to consider the case of Germany. One could argue that for many years Germany was running a current-account surplus and accumulating foreign exchange that was not yielding her much return. Surely, it was said, as a nation she would have been better off raising absorption to the level of real income and offsetting the consequent inflationary pressure with an appreciation. It is not difficult to think of all the politically attractive things that the government of the Federal Republic could have done with increased funds at its disposal, whether to increase expenditures or cut taxes. But the appreciation would have lowered real profits in the tradable sector, and possibly eventually in the economy as a whole. Real wages, of course, would have risen, doubly so because of the government expenditure increases or tax cuts. Finally after-tax profits need not have fallen; for example, the fall in profits owing to the switching effect could have been offset by a cut in corporate tax as part of the absorption-increasing policy. But it is clear enough that firms in the export industries did not take the latter effect into account and assessed that the net result of these policies would leave them worse off. German reluctance to appreciate sufficiently was to some extent a consequence of these fears of exporters.

Real-Wage Resistance

It is often said that a devaluation will lead to a compensating rise in money-wages designed to avoid a fall in real wages, and that this 'real-wage resistance' will negate the effects of a devaluation, making it pointless. Switching is simply not possible as a result of policy. The only way to get an improvement in the balance of payments is to reduce absorption appropriately, even at the cost of unemployment. The unemployment consequent on this cut in absorption is the true cost of downward inflexibility of real wages. Eventually a real-wage fall may be induced by the unemployment; it certainly will not be induced by the devaluation. This is an extreme way of putting the argument, but let us analyse its implications in more detail. We shall consider the case where both the absorption cut involves some fall in real total wages and a switching policy, such as devaluation, leads to a further fall because non-tradables are labour-intensive relative to tradables.

Let us first suppose that money-wages have stayed constant, and the appropriate disabsorption policy combined with devaluation has brought about external balance while retaining internal balance. Real wages—interpreted in the broad sense of *total* real wages— have fallen for the two reasons mentioned. After a while money-wages rise to compensate for that part of the real-wage cut brought about by the devaluation itself. The switching effect will then be completely reversed, the prices of non-tradables rising to the same extent as the prices of tradables. Given that expenditure is now equal to income, some unemployment and external imbalance will return.

But this is not all. Money-wages may also rise to compensate for the effect of the expenditure reduction. For example, suppose that the expenditure reduction was brought about by raising tax rates on wage-earners. The pre-tax (earned) money-wage may then be pushed up to bring the post-tax real-wage back to where it was originally. This extra rise in the pre-tax money-wage would have an additional switching effect, actually raising the prices of non-tradables relative to tradables *above* where they were in the very first place. This is the same effect as if there had been an appreciation with constant money wages.

If there is indeed this real-wage resistance it may not be possible to attain both internal and external balance. Essentially the point is that the real wage that is apparently insisted on by wage-earners exceeds the marginal product of labour at full employment.

The matter can be resolved in three ways. Firstly the real wage actually paid out can be supplemented by borrowing from abroad, so that the total income of the wage-earner—including social wage, subsidies, and so on—is at the desired level even when the wage paid by employers is at the lower level appropriate to full employment. This is the solution of an external deficit. Secondly, the external deficit can be eliminated and employment reduced to the level appropriate to that real wage, perhaps in the hope that eventually the unemployment will lead to a reduction in the real wage. A third solution is that there be an offsetting domestic re-distribution of income towards wages: for example, profits might be taxed in order to subsidize wages. This assumes that real profits, unlike real wages, are not resistant to a reduction.

Each of these resolutions has its problems. An external deficit involves interest earnings foregone on owned reserves or interest payments made on loans raised and, in any case, may not be able to go on for ever. The costs of unemployment are obvious. And the third solution may involve various distortions and disincentives, as well as reducing funds for investment. I shall come back to the third solution in a moment, but first some general remarks about the relationship between wage rigidity and the uses of a devaluation should be made.

In the context of the present type of model, a devaluation has a role when there is money-wage rigidity downwards (or a similar rigidity of the money prices of non-traded goods) provided that, at the same time, the real-wage is flexible. This is a particularly important matter to appreciate. If the money-wage were not rigid downwards there would be no need for a deliberate switching policy, since switching would be automatic in response to unemployment in the labour market. Devaluation substitutes for a fall in money-wages, and if money-wages would fall in any case there is no need for a devaluation. These are both ways of attaining the fall in real wages that is normally necessary. On the other hand, if the real-wage were inflexible downwards a devaluation would be ineffective. To make devaluation *necessary* money-wages have to be *in*flexible, and to make it *effective* real wages have to be flexible.

The third solution mentioned a moment ago involved subsidizing wages in order to maintain full employment with external balance. This could be done in an *open* way or in an *indirect* way.

The *open* way is to tax profits or rents in order to subsidize wage-earners or the employment of labour. It may, of course, not be feasible to subsidize wages to the extent necessary. The revenue yielded by a profits tax at the maximum revenue level may simply be insufficient. Furthermore, the desired or target real-wage may not be a constant: it may continuously run ahead of the willingness of society to make the transfer. It is not a policy that I am advocating, but it is a possibility for dealing with a short-term problem.

There are also *indirect* ways of approaching this problem. Here it is particularly relevant to consider the use of trade policies as an indirect way of subsidizing wages at the expense of profits and rents. This is a popular approach. It is sometimes said that while a devaluation will lead to a compensating rise in money-wages, a well-designed set of tariffs or import quotas—which are also switching devices—may not do so. In theory this is at least possible. For example, if a country's import-competing goods tend to be labour-intensive and its export industries capital-intensive, the imposition of a tariff instead of a devaluation will shift incomes from profits to wages, at least when one compares the tariff with the devaluation outcome. The tariff is then an indirect way of taxing profits to subsidize wages.

A tariff system that involves low or zero duties on goods consumed mainly by workers (food), and high duties on goods consumed by others (luxury goods) may also have this effect. Thus some recent advocates of import quotas in Britain were concerned that a devaluation would raise food prices and that this would provoke money-wage increases, the implicit assumption being that there is real-wage resistance, that food is particularly a wage-good, that the familiar distortions created are unimportant, and that the income redistribution away from the non-wage sector thus brought about would have no adverse effects (such as a reduction in investment) that need to be taken into account. Therefore they preferred restrictions on manufactured imports to devaluation, given that some switching was necessary to maintain full employment. I should add that some of my colleagues and I argued against this. In particular we argued that even if the basic assumptions were granted, and it were desired to subsidize wages by subsidizing food consumption, direct food subsidies paid for out of government revenue are preferable to the highly indirect approach of import quotas.

REFERENCES

The analysis of devaluation with money-wage rigidity is presented more rigorously in R. W. Jones and W. M. Corden, 'Devaluation, Non-Flexible Prices, and the Trade Balance for a Small Country', *Canadian Journal of Economics*, 9 (February 1976), 150–61. See also R. Dornbusch, 'Alternative Price Stabilization Rules and the Effects of Exchange Rate Changes', *Manchester School*, 43 (September 1975), 275–97.

3

MONEY, THE MONETARY APPROACH, CAPITAL MOVEMENTS, AND PORTFOLIO BALANCE

MONEY has played rather a shadowy role in the discussion so far. It has been a standard of value in terms of which wages or the prices of non-tradables may be rigid, and we have talked about its price relative to other moneys—the exchange rate. But nothing explicit has been said in the previous two chapters about the quantity of money. How can one talk about devaluation and balance-of-payments problems without bringing in the quantity of money? Has it been Hamlet without the Prince?

I shall certainly not spend much time here expounding the monetary approach to balance of payments theory. This has been done rather often by now, and the literature is vast. All I want to do is to bring monetary matters into the basic model and to relate some aspects of the monetary approach to it. While initially I shall continue to assume that there are no private capital movements, they will be brought in eventually. Finally I want to ask a rather fundamental question—the answer to which possibly throws doubts on our basic model—namely 'What really is a balance of payments problem?'

Monetary Implications of a Deficit

Let us begin with the monetary implications of the initial balance of payments deficit in our—by now—familiar story. An excess of absorption over income means either that cash balances (meaning currency plus deposits) are being run down or that new credit is being created to the extent of the deficit. In the case of a run-down of cash balances, members of the private sector are making a portfolio adjustment. They have too much money, and want to get rid of some of it, hence spending it on goods and services. The run-down in domestic deposits causes an equivalent run-down in foreign exchange. Presumably this process will naturally come to an end when the portfolio adjustment has taken place.

In the case of domestic-credit creation one could tell a simple story as follows. The quantity of money that is held does not increase because people have all the cash balances they wish to hold. (If the demand for cash balances is increasing at the same time, we are talking here about the excess of credit creation over the increase in demand for cash balances.) The increase in money resulting from the new credit is then immediately matched by a decrease owing to the deficit. Of course, if the economy has not fully adjusted to the flow of new credit there may be some increase in money supply as a result, dishoarding of the extra balances taking place with a lag. One might go more deeply into the question of what motivates the private non-banking sector in incurring extra liabilities—which must be so when it is borrowing from the banking system and then spending part or all of the proceeds. Presumably the inducement was a fall in the interest rate, or alternatively the sector had initially an excess demand for borrowing for consumption or real investment. If the interest rate falls there is likely to be some rise in money holdings.

In any case, there can only be a continuous balance of payments deficit if there is a continuous increase in credit. As far as the banking system is concerned, its domestic assets steadily increase, the result of credit creation, while the foreign assets decrease, the result of the decline in foreign-exchange reserves. This process can only go on as long as there are any foreign reserves left.

The remedy for a deficit seems simple and obvious when put in this way: stop creating credit. Stop attempting to increase the supply of money faster than the demand for it is increasing! This recommendation to stop creating credit is indeed what, at this stage of the argument, is meant when we say that absorption must be reduced until it equals income, and leaving aside any changes in the level of cash balances people wish to hold. It should be noted that no distinction need be made between the private and public sector in all this. The credit could be fed into the system through the private sector via the commercial banking system, or it could finance a fiscal deficit. A problem, of course, remains, whether for the private or the public sector, namely the problem of cutting expenditure to match the reduction in credit.

The Cash-Balance Effect of Devaluation

Let us continue to assume for the moment that money wages are rigid downwards, though real wages are flexible. When the credit expansion is reduced or eliminated in order to improve the balance of payments and to stop the decline in foreign-exchange reserves there is, as before, a need for devaluation in order to switch the absorption and production patterns, and so avoid excess supply in the market for non-tradables. This is our familiar 'two-instruments two-targets' story. Similarly, a devaluation would be necessary if a decumulation of cash balances by the private sector came to an end.

Now we come to a central theme of the monetary approach. The devaluation will itself have an effect on the desire to accumulate cash balances. Normally the devaluation will raise the average domestic price-level (if the price of non-tradables actually falls, as it did in one of the models, a devaluation may conceivably *not* raise the price level). With a higher domestic price-level a given nominal money supply will represent a lower real money supply. People will then wish to reconstitute their cash balances and so, for a limited period, their expenditures will run below their incomes. Thus a devaluation gives rise to a balance of payments surplus, assuming that previously people were content with their cash balances or that domestic credit creation has ceased.

This cash balance effect of a devaluation can be combined with our main story, where we start with a deficit, and where there is downward rigidity of money wages or prices of non-traded goods. It should be noted that the monetary models of the balance of payments generally assume downward flexibility of wages, so they would not tell the story to follow. (In addition, the monetary models commonly assume that the balance of payments was in equilibrium to start with.) I am here combining a feature of our basic model with a feature of the monetary model.

First, suppose that initially there was a balance of payments deficit because of credit expansion. It is proposed to put an end to this deficit. If credit creation ceased, absorption would fall, and with a constant exchange rate, this would lead to unemployment. To maintain internal balance a devaluation is then necessary.

The complication is that the devaluation itself will increase the demand for nominal cash balances, and hence bring about a fall in absorption. If credit creation ceased completely, and simultaneously there was a devaluation, the country would actually go into surplus. The appropriate policy would then seem to be for credit creation to cease gradually. Once the country has devalued, enough new credit should be created to meet the extra demand for nominal balances resulting from the devaluation. Absorption would be reduced immediately to the level appropriate to flow external balance (where there is no net hoarding). Initially only part of the reduction in absorption would be caused by the reduction in credit creation; the other part would be caused by the rebuilding of real balances following the devaluation.

Next, suppose that initially there was a deficit because people were running down excess cash balances. As they approach the desired level of cash balances and so reduce absorption the exchange rate needs to be devalued for internal balance to be maintained. But this devaluation will actually raise the demand for cash balances, and hence will speed up the decline in absorption. The country could even go into surplus for a period, actually building up its cash balances, before finally reaching external balance with the exchange rate appropriate to external balance and the level of cash balances appropriate to the price-level yielded by that exchange rate.

This seems to me the way in which devaluation and the cash-balance effect fit into our basic model. Devaluation is still necessary because of rigid money wages. The cash-balance effect is a by-product of devaluation which needs to be taken into account either if we wish to predict the balance-of-payments effects of various given policies, such as reducing credit creation while maintaining internal balance, or if we wish to set external and internal balance as policy targets.

The Role of Devaluation in Monetary Models

As I have just said, in most monetary models of the balance of payments, money wages are assumed to be flexible, so that devaluation does not have this internal balance role. Has it then another role? It is usually seen as an arbitrary policy action which raises the domestic price-level, so reduces the real money supply, and thus yields a temporary surplus as the real money supply is rebuilt. Similarly, an appreciation would raise the real money supply and yield a temporary deficit. Devaluation builds up the foreign-exchange reserves and appreciation reduces them.

In fact credit contraction can achieve the same effects on the external situation as a devaluation; the domestic assets of the banking system would then contract as the foreign ones expanded. Similarly credit creation could achieve the same effects as an appreciation. It is rather interesting to note that the exchange rate has become the instrument determining the level of absorption, while price flexibility brings about automatic switching. The exchange rate has replaced credit policy as the instrument for varying absorption.

The question still remains why the exchange rate should be used for this purpose. Why not use credit policy? If the object of policy is to increase the foreign-exchange reserves, a case can perhaps be made. It is presumably easier to devalue and raise the general price-level, and so neatly impose a capital levy on cash balances, than it is to contract credit. But the question then arises why it should be desired to attain a particular level of foreign-exchange reserves. If the aim is to meet the potential needs of the private sector then presumably the private sector will increase its cash balances when it wants to do so, and so generate the necessary external surplus and foreign-exchange. The aim may be rather to meet the potential needs of the public sector, so that the devaluation is really just a capital levy, the revenue of which goes into the country's foreign-exchange reserves. Finally, if the object of policy is to reduce the foreign-exchange reserves there seems little reason to prefer appreciation to a credit expansion.

Perhaps one should have some doubts about the role of the exchange rate as a way of regulating absorption and hence the level of foreign-exchange reserves. But there is one other role which, surely, must become its main purpose once it is presumed not to affect employment. This is the objective of regulating the domestic price-level, and in particular to insulate the economy from foreign price fluctuations. This is an aspect to which we shall come in the next chapters.

Introducing Private Capital Movements

In the previous two chapters and up to this point in the present chapter I have assumed that there are no private-capital inflows or outflows. Once we allow for such capital movements the concept of 'external balance' must be looked at again. For the moment I shall simply define external balance as a situation where the official foreign-exchange reserves do not alter. One approach would be to take private-capital flows as given exogenously. External balance would then be the achievement of a current-account deficit equal to the given capital account surplus. The analysis yielded by our basic model would not need to be altered at all. But this is clearly not satisfactory.

The complication that needs to be introduced is that various policies which alter absorption will also alter private-capital flows. I shall look first at monetary policy and later at fiscal policy.

Let me first suppose that there is continuous domestic credit expansion, and simplify a little to bring out the main points. The credit creation will, as before, lead to some increase in consumption and hence absorption, as the beneficiaries of the credit seek to avoid building up excessive cash balances. The rate of interest will fall. This was our earlier story, and will lead, as before, to a current-account deficit. But this time, some of the extra money may also be transformed into foreign claims—securities, bonds, and bills—in an attempt to maintain a portfolio balance between cash and claims. The import of claims—or export of capital—will then lead to a deficit on capital account.

Thus the effect on the balance of payments as a whole—the official-settlements balance—will be the same as before, for given credit creation, but the effect on the current account will be less, since some of the effect will be manifested in the capital account. It remains true that to stop the decline in foreign-exchange reserves, domestic-credit creation has to cease. Furthermore, switching will still be needed to maintain internal balance if the current-account deficit is eliminated. But the extent of switching required will be less.

In this account I have combined a portfolio-balance operation—maintaining a balance between cash and claims—with what might be called a portfolio-adjustment operation—gradually adjusting the size of the total portfolio, consisting of cash and claims together, to the level of income. When cash is increased I have supposed that some of it is converted into claims (portfolio balancing) and some into goods (portfolio adjustment), the first leading to a capital-account deficit and the second to a current-account deficit.

But one might suppose that portfolio balancing takes place very quickly and portfolio adjustment gradually.

To make this distinction, let us consider the effects of a once-for-all increase in cash balances. The first, almost instantaneous, stage is then for part of these balances to be converted into claims, so yielding a capital-account deficit. At this stage the current account is not affected. The next, more prolonged, stage is for the remainder of the original increase in cash balances *and* the increase in claims that resulted from the first stage to be gradually converted into goods, hence yielding a current-account deficit partly financed by a capital-account surplus. The main implication is that an accumulation of foreign claims resulting from an increase in cash balances would only be temporary—at least in this model.

I have assumed here that an increase in cash (credit) is seen as a rise in net wealth by the private sector. This would be so when extra cash is distributed via a public deficit as taxation reductions or income transfers. But when monetary expansion is by open market operations one can argue that there is no rise in net wealth; credit expansion then affects the current account only through the stimulus that a fall in interest rates gives to investment.

Let me now turn briefly to fiscal policy. This seems to raise an interesting issue as to what we mean by external balance. Let us suppose government expenditure is increased, yielding a budget deficit. This will lead to an increase in absorption and a current-account deficit. If it were wholly financed by credit creation there would be no effect on the capital account. The foreign-exchange reserves would fall by the extent of the current-account deficit. But, instead, let us suppose that we have a *pure* fiscal policy, hence unaccompanied by credit expansion.

A budget deficit that is not financed by credit creation must be financed on the capital market. Consider first the extreme case where the interest rate is given to the country from outside. The budget deficit will then lead to an equivalent import of capital. If we define this as private-capital inflow, the current-account deficit will have been balanced by a capital-account surplus. The foreign-exchange reserves will remain unchanged. The government's bonds may have been sold to domestic residents, but of course there is a single world capital market, so in fact the government of this small country has borrowed from foreigners to finance its budget deficit.

If we defined *any* borrowing by the government or central bank as being accommodating, and thus made no distinction between government borrowing on the market and borrowing from the central bank, the latter causing the foreign-exchange reserves to run down, our original story would not be altered at all: a budget deficit would have led to an equivalent balance-of-payments deficit irrespective of whether it was financed by credit creation or the government had to go on the capital market to finance it. The latter approach seems to me the sensible one.

If the interest rate rises as a result of the extra borrowing by the government, not all the bonds the government sells will end up abroad. Some will be held domestically in place of money, so that (owing to reduced money holdings) there will be some net fall in the foreign-exchange reserves. In other words, the capital-account surplus induced by the budget deficit will be less than the current-account deficit.

So far the analysis of our basic model does not seem to have been significantly affected. If a country is running a balance-of-payments deficit that is causing its foreign-exchange reserves to run down or that is financed by official borrowing abroad, it must have been induced by credit creation or by a fiscal deficit, or both (aside from private cash balances being run down). If this balance-of-payments deficit is to stop, absorption must fall. If there is downward rigidity of money wages but not real wages a switching policy will then be needed to maintain internal balance. What then is new as a result of introducing private capital movements? It is this: when there is credit creation there is likely to be (at least temporarily) some accumulation of foreign claims by the private sector, and to that extent the increase in absorption associated with a given official-settlements deficit will be less than when there is no opportunity for such inflow, or when the same balance-of-payments deficit is brought about by a fiscal deficit not financed by credit creation.

The models in this field, originating with Meade and Mundell, have a variable interest rate as a crucial ingredient, and I have also referred to this. More needs to be said about the rate of interest. The sensible thing to assume is that as the country accumulates more and more private foreign claims their prices go up—that is, the interest rate falls as capital flows out, and vice versa. It has come to be realized that it is not very sensible to assume that the interest rate is some constant function of capital outflows and inflows per period of time—which was indeed an assumption in many of the original models in this area. Rather, it may be thought of as a function of accumulated flows, a function that may move over time with growth abroad.

The main point is that credit creation will lower the rate of interest, and pure fiscal expansion will raise it. This follows from the standard closed economy Keynesian LM–IS model. These interest rate changes—which may only be short-run—will affect investment within the country: the supply of domestic claims will rise as the interest rate falls, and investment becomes more profitable. All this need not be spelt out. It need only be noted that in the case of credit creation the cash-balance effect on absorption will be strengthened by an investment effect—credit creation increasing absorption for *two* reasons—but the general analysis earlier will not be greatly altered.

When Is There a Balance-of-Payments Problem? A Simple Case

I come to a final issue that has been hovering in the background. The whole question of what the meaning is of 'external balance' and when there is a balance-of-payments 'problem' has so far been skated over, as indeed it has been skated over in much of the pre-monetarist literature on balance-of-payments theory. It has been *target theory* rather than *optimizing theory*. Balance-of-payments 'equilibrium' has usually been defined in flow terms as some target, such as current-account balance or official-settlements balance.

The elementary model that seems to be implicit in much discussion of balance-of-payments problems is as follows. We have a non-growing economy where there is no domestic net investment. All absorption is for consumption and maintaining capital intact. Absorption exceeds output because of domestic-credit creation, so that the foreign-exchange reserves are running down. Thus the country is disinvesting. It is 'living beyond its means'. This is the balance-of-payments problem. The target is to stop it. The model will have to be generalized later, but it is sufficient to bring out some important issues. What really is the problem? We need to go deeper into this.

There seem to be three types of problem:

(1) The monetary authorities may, in some sense, not know

what they are doing, or may be doing what they really don't want to do. The country's reserves may be falling below the optimal reserves level, whatever it is, but the authorities have misjudged the need to do something. This might be called the 'misjudgement problem'.

(2) The reserves may be falling because they are above the optimal level, and the country is going through a deliberate stock-readjustment process. The problem then is that the current level of consumption will have to be reduced once the stock adjustment has been completed; cutting consumption is painful, and the problem is the anticipation of this pain. This is the 'consumption adjustment problem'.

(3) Finally, there is the 'switching problem'. Foreign-exchange reserves cannot fall for ever, and in any case it may be decided by the authorities that they shall cease falling, or that the rate of fall shall be slowed down. Hence the existing *flow* situation with its high absorption level will have to alter; the country has to move towards a new flow situation (I hesitate to use the word 'equilibrium') where absorption equals output. But this involves switching, whether brought about by exchange-rate adjustment or by money-wage flexibility, and switching brings with it problems.

The switching problem might be regarded as having two aspects. The more important aspect is that switching is induced by a relative-price change, and a relative-price change leads to changes in income distribution. The problem is that incomes of some sections of the community will have to fall as a consequence of the relative-price change, and this may create hardship and resistances. The second aspect is that switching involves resource reallocation and hence the familiar adjustment costs for the parties concerned. The switching problem would also exist if there were a balance-of-payments surplus which had to be eliminated, possibly by initiative from the deficit countries with which the home country trades. Switching is always a problem, especially if disequilibrium relative prices have been allowed to persist for a considerable run of years, as they sometimes were in the days of the Bretton Woods par-value system.

If the reason for the deficit is a run-down in cash balances, say by firms, then the problems are essentially the same. First, the managements of the firms may not know what they are doing or find themselves doing something—namely over-spending—that is giving them sleepless nights as they see bankruptcy on the horizon. Secondly, the firms may be going through a deliberate stock adjustment process, and the current level of expenditure may have to be reduced soon, the anticipation of which also gives rise to disturbed nights in high places. Finally, because cash balances cannot and will not run down forever, there is the same switching problem as before.

Some of the monetarist discussions convey the impression that a deficit cannot be a 'problem' because it must eventually come to an end. It simply represents a stock adjustment, and how can the process of adjusting stocks to desired levels be a 'problem'? I suppose that one might ask how anything in the economy can be a problem. If everyone does what he wants to do, and knows what he is doing, and adjusts to changing circumstances, where is the problem? The answer, of course, is that some private people, firms, and governments may make mistakes in adjustment, and even when they do not, the process of adjusting—whether it requires eventually cutting consumption or altering price ratios to induce switching and adjusting to the new price signals—is a problem to the people and institutions concerned.

Possibly one might make a distinction between *private* problems and *public* problems. I shall come back to this line of thought again later, but the general idea could be that the whole balance-of-payments issue is a public-policy issue, not a matter of efficient business or household management. One should therefore just assume for the purpose of discussing balance-of-payments issues that the private sector knows what it is doing, and what is good for it, as far as its spending and saving decisions are concerned. The switching problem will then still arise irrespective of whether the reason for a payments deficit is a run-down in private-cash balances or credit creation; but the other two problems only exist as so-called balance-of-payments-policy problems when the reason for the deficit is credit creation (involving some element of public or central-bank deficit).

One final point can be made at this stage. External balance can clearly not be defined wholly in flow terms, and certainly not as a situation of zero deficit and surplus in the balance of payments. External balance is essentially a stock concept now (though it will have a flow element in it when there is growth). This true external balance one could call *stock* external balance. But at any point in time a certain *flow* external-balance target will be implied by the combination of the stock external-balance level and the actual situation the country is in. Flow external balance may well be a deficit or a surplus. This flow target will change over time and will be aimed at gradually achieving the stock balance. Flow external balance is then the proximate target, and can be fed into the basic model as a guide to the immediate absorption and switching policies required. When one looks at the matter in this way, one sees that the basic model continues to be useful, especially for the short run, but is certainly incomplete.

I come now to further issues which are possibly more destructive of the basic model.

When Is There a Balance-of-Payments Problem? A Broader View

The simple model that I have just used has some obvious limitations. In this model there were no private capital movements, and indeed no public borrowing. And all the country's absorption of goods and services was used for consumption and maintaining capital intact, and none for net investment. The model needs to be broadened. If the decline in foreign-exchange reserves were arrested by inducing increased private borrowing abroad, there would be no change in net investment for the nation as a whole, and the country might continue to live beyond its means. Similarly, if the decline were arrested by a reduction in absorption brought about by failing to keep real capital intact, there would be no change in net disinvestment. Just looking at the foreign-exchange reserves does not show whether the country is 'living beyond its means' and will eventually have to cut consumption. Nor does it show whether the portfolio of assets is satisfactorily distributed.

The most general model is one where there are many different forms of consumption and many different forms of assets. For each decision-making unit in the economy of a country—including the government and the central bank, perhaps, as separate units— there is an optimal pattern of consumption at any time, an optimal balanced portfolio of assets, as well as an optimal total of these assets. Each unit has a flow demand and supply of assets which reflects a process of approaching the optimal portfolio. Tastes, technologies, external conditions—including the tastes and techno- logies of foreign countries—change. So flow demands and supplies alter not only because the units are working towards optimal stocks and portfolios of stocks but also because of these taste and technology changes. Assets include money, bonds, and rights to ownership of real capital.

For each flow, whether of goods, services, or financial assets, there is then a domestic demand and supply determined in this sort of way. When there is excess demand, the good, service, etc., is imported. What then is 'the' balance of payments? This is the issue that has been much discussed in connection with the United States balance-of-payments. The aim has been, at least implicitly, to define a balance-of-payments deficit or surplus in such a way that it focuses on a 'problem', presumably a policy problem. For all goods, services, and financial assets, including money, the sum of excess demands and supplies adds up to zero, so that we can get any balance-of-payments figure we want by choosing the appropriate group of goods, services, and assets. If one takes goods and services together with net-property income, remittances, and government grants, one gets the balance-of-payments on current account, for example. There are various other combinations, yielding such concepts as the liquidity balance and the official-settlements balance. But what are the principles involved?

The monetary theory of the balance-of-payments argues that the balance-of-payments is essentially a monetary phenomenon. Its advocates would define a balance-of-payments deficit as being equal to an excess-flow supply of money. This is also how it came out in our simpler models: the balance-of-payments deficit was equal to the excess of domestic-credit creation (extra supply) over the increased demand for cash balances (extra demand). But it is really rather an arbitrary definition, and does not necessarily focus on the 'problem'. Suppose that the private sector has a zero financial balance. Now, when the government of a country borrows short term on the world capital market to finance a fiscal deficit we would say that there is a short-term capital inflow, and possibly no effect on the monetarists' payments balance. On the other hand, when the central bank creates domestic money to finance the fiscal deficit, and then has to run down its foreign-exchange reserves (which have been invested short term on the same world market), the monetarists' balance of payments has gone into deficit.

In a most general sense, there are problems if assets as a whole—

or particular assets, notably liquid assets—are running down too fast, so that consumption will in due course have to decline; or if the portfolio of assets is not right, and it is not currently in the process of moving in the right direction. Perhaps most importantly, there is a switching problem if flow equilibrium requires relative prices to change and hence income distribution to alter, and so causes some real factor incomes to fall.

It has to be admitted that to look at excess demands or supplies of any particular group of goods, services, and assets—which is what balance-of-payments data give us—will not really tell us about these problems or necessarily even focus on them. There may be no excess demand for money, and yet the country may be 'living beyond its means'—or non-optimally below them—its private-asset portfolio may be too liquid or not liquid enough, and there may certainly be need for switching.

The monetary approach hinges on a reasonable definition of 'money', since the balance of payments is described as the excess demand or supply of money, so defined. The supply of money is seen as the key policy variable, and excess supply is, presumably, seen as a problem.

Alternatively, one might regard the monetary approach not so much as focusing on a 'problem' but as providing a way of explaining changes in official reserves (gold, SDRs, and foreign exchange). The approach thus accepts a common view as to which figures are important and provides a way of interpreting them. The question then becomes whether this 'reserves balance' is a significant concept, and whether a method of analysis that focuses on it represents the best kind of simplification. The strongest argument one can make for it as the key figure is that it focuses on the central bank's principal portfolio problem. The difficulty here is that the country, and more particularly the public sector, consists of more than the central bank.

In the case of countries other than the United States and the United Kingdom, the widely used 'balance on official settlements' is more or less equivalent to what I have called the 'reserves balance'. The official-settlements balance is the balance settled by changes in a country's own official reserves *and* by changes in holdings of the country's currency by foreign official agencies. But the latter element is important only for the two reserve-currency countries. I shall suggest in Chapter 9 that the official-settlements-balance concept is not a useful concept for the reserve-currency countries because of this latter element.

In the search for simple approaches one could think of at least one other. One could focus on liquid assets and liabilities. One then defines the balance-of-payments as the so-called 'basic balance', which is the balance on current account and long-term capital, leaving liquid capital movements, whether private or public, and reserve changes, as the residual items. A shift from long-term borrowing to short-term borrowing would worsen the balance-of-payments; a decline in foreign-exchange reserves which finances an accumulation of private liquid claims leaves it unchanged. One makes no distinction between public and private assets and liabilities. There is *stock* external balance when the level of liquid assets minus liabilities is just right in relation to consumption levels and long-term assets, while *flow* external balance represents the changing target level designed eventually to attain stock balance. There is a 'problem' when the stock is too low, when there is a danger it might even 'run out', and when flow changes are required to get closer to stock balance.

One can thus make a case for regarding the maintenance of a preferred stock of international liquidity by a country as an object of policy, defining the balance-of-payments as a guide to this policy. The general idea behind this is that one wants to provide for emergencies. If a famine or a revolution hit the country, could it live beyond its means for a while? And taking into account liquid liabilities, one also wants to know whether the country might suddenly be required to make drastic adjustments because other countries wish to draw on their liquid assets.

The objection to the measure is that if there is an international short-term capital market and a country is 'credit-worthy' it does not need liquid assets, or at least only needs them to the extent that this is the way of becoming credit-worthy. But in principle credit-worthiness need not depend on the ownership of liquid assets (minus liabilities). The ownership of long-term assets that have some reasonable market value may be enough, as may a reputation as a non-defaulting debtor. In practice it is not really possible to distinguish liquid from non-liquid capital transactions. An investor might buy foreign long-dated securities, but intend to sell them shortly. Changes in direct-investment flows are usually regarded as long-term capital movements, but include volatile short-term flows.

Any distinction between long-term and short-term flows is bound
to be arbitrary, and for this reason the distinction has recently been
abolished in the U.S. balance-of-payments statistics.

Does the Balance of Payments Matter at all?

Finally, one could adopt a rather radical approach, but one which
seems to me well worth considering. One focuses on the distinction between the public and the private sector. This raises issues
already discussed. One could argue that the private sector can take
care of itself, and that so-called policy problems only concern the
public sector, including of course the central bank. One assumes
that any decision by the private sector to run down assets, or to change
its asset portfolio, perhaps from short term to long term, is optimal,
or at least does not present a problem for public policy. If private
firms choose to increase their spending and finance this by borrowing abroad, and so generate a current-account deficit, this does
not call for any public policy concern or intervention. One need not
assume that the current-account deficit indicates any problem.
Similarly, one need not regard a current-account surplus resulting
from a decision to invest in liquid balances rather than in fixed
capital equipment as particularly cheering.

It may indeed be desirable for governments to help the private
sector make its various decisions on the basis of good information
and forecasts. Furthermore, various divergencies between social
and private costs and benefits should be corrected, so that private
decisions are made on the basis of price signals that indicate social
and not just private costs and returns. But there is no need for
concern with particular quantitative outcomes, and certainly not
for any public-policy quantitative targets.

By contrast, public policy *is* concerned with the public sector. In
the public sector one does not assume that a run-down in assets or a
shift in their composition, perhaps towards less liquid assets, is
optimal. One sees potential problems and makes statistical
calculations to focus on these. In that case one would not focus on
total national absorption, but only on *public* consumption and
investment. One would then relate this to the *public* decumulation
of financial assets and liabilities of all kinds, whether foreign or
domestically held.

The radical implication of this approach is as follows. Since the
various components of the balance of payments show the results of

both public and private demands and supplies (except for the supply of money, which is wholly publicly supplied), balance-of-payments figures would not really be the relevant figures to look at. The current-account deficit of a country is the sum of the private financial deficit (excess of investment over savings) and the public deficit. If the current-account deficit increases this may be because the private deficit has risen—which is not a matter for public-policy concern—or because the public deficit has risen—which may indeed be a matter for concern. But the balance-of-payments figures in themselves will not tell one whether there is a problem. One must go directly to the public-sector (including central-bank) figures, so making the balance-of-payments figures redundant.

Like all simple, and perhaps radical, ideas, there are qualifications to this. One qualification is that the public sector is not separate from its citizens. If a country were faced with an emergency the state could first draw on its own liquid assets. But if the private sector also has foreign liquid assets, one cannot ignore these. The state could tax the private sector and so draw on the private assets at one remove. A more important qualification is that sometimes the private sector borrows abroad subject to explicit or implicit government guarantees. Alternatively, it may borrow domestically from state-owned banks at rates of interest which are below the world interest rates at which these banks, in turn, have to borrow to finance their domestic loans. In all these cases one could then argue that the sharp distinction between the public and the private sector is as arbitrary as the various other sharp distinctions on which different concepts of balance-of-payments deficits rest.

REFERENCES

There are numerous articles presenting the monetary approach, which originated with David Hume and had its modern revival in the writings of Robert Mundell. Many of the relevant papers have been collected in Jacob A. Frenkel and Harry G. Johnson (eds.), *The Monetary Approach to the Balance of Payments*, Allen & Unwin, London, 1976. A particularly neat exposition using the 'traded–non-traded-goods' approach, and so fitting in with the exposition here, is R. Dornbusch, 'Devaluation, Money and Non-traded Goods', *American Economic Review*, 63 (December 1973), 871–80 (also reprinted in Jacob A. Frenkel and Harry G. Johnson (eds.), *The Monetary Approach to the Balance of Payments*). The section in this chapter on 'Introducing Private Capital Movements' was greatly influenced by Jacob A. Frenkel and Carlos A. Rodriguez, 'Portfolio Equilibrium and the Balance of Payments: A Monetary Approach', *American Economic Review*, 65 (September 1975), 674–87. A valuable critical review of the monetary approach is in Marina v. N. Whitman, 'Global Monetarism and the Monetary Approach to the Balance of Payments', *Brookings Papers on Economic Activity*, 1975 (3), 491–536. Finally, an excellent survey which includes a review of the relevant empirical literature is M. E. Kreinin and L. H. Officer, *The Monetary Approach to the Balance of Payments: A Survey*, Studies in International Finance, 43, Princeton, 1978.

INFLATION AND
EXCHANGE RATES

4

INFLATION AND THE
EXCHANGE-RATE SYSTEM:
A SYMMETRICAL APPROACH

THE aim in this chapter is to analyse the relationship between inflation and the exchange-rate system. Is a system of fixed or of flexible rates more inflationary? If one cannot give a clear answer to this question, what, at least, are the relevant considerations?

Many answers have been given to this question. Some people point out that a devaluation is obviously inflationary because it raises the domestic prices of traded goods, so that a system that provokes a devaluation must be conducive to inflation. Others might point out that inflation brings about devaluation, and not vice versa. And, in any case, if devaluation is inflationary, then presumably appreciation is deflationary. Various asymmetries are noted. Some argue that a flexible system causes relative prices to change, and because of ratchet effects, this has a net inflationary effect (since money prices go up, but never down); others derive exactly the opposite conclusion from the same asymmetrical response of money prices: they argue that in a fixed-rate system deficit countries do not drop their prices while surplus countries have to raise theirs, so that the net result of the *fixed*-rate system is to raise the world price-level.

The immediate interest in the question is the superficial correlation between world inflation and the floating of exchange rates. The floating rate system began in March 1973 (though there was an earlier period of floating from August to December 1971), and in 1976, all the industrialized countries were floating either independently or as part of the D-mark-dominated 'snake'. At the same time world inflation accelerated in 1973 and 1974, though the great world inflation certainly got under way before then. It is therefore natural that people should ask whether the floating caused the inflation, or vice versa, or indeed whether there was a common third cause.

I might as well give the brief answer to the latter question straight away. Certainly the great inflation was generated in the fixed-rate system, but the divergent inflation rates which developed made some degree of exchange-rate flexibility inevitable. This need for exchange-rate flexibility was possibly strengthened by the various effects of the oil-price rise. Thus the pre-October 1973 inflation combined with the effects of the oil-price rise caused floating, not vice versa. At the same time, floating allowed inflation rates to diverge sharply in 1974 and 1975. In the absence of exchange-rate flexibility the inflation rates of some of the high-inflation countries such as Britain and Italy would certainly not have been as high.

But let me proceed to a systematic approach. I shall begin with a very simple model in which there are no asymmetries. These will be introduced in Chapter 5. The initial analysis will not apply to the special case of the reserve-currency country. I shall come to that special case in Chapter 6.

The Story of an Inflation-Prone Country: The Fixed-Exchange-Rate Situation

Let us suppose that there is a given world rate of inflation of, say, 5 per cent. To start with, the country under consideration also has an inflation rate of 5 per cent. Its money supply is growing at that rate, its prices and wages are growing at that rate, and it is in current-account balance. To simplify, there are initially no net-capital flows. Furthermore, there are no structural changes, such as changes in demand patterns, which would make balance-of-payments equilibrium compatible with a rate of inflation in that country which differs from the world rate of inflation.

Now a government enters office in this country eager to spend more without raising extra taxes; or it wishes to bring down unemployment. I shall call it an inflation-prone country. At the same time the country is firmly committed to a fixed exchange rate.

Let us suppose that, one way or another, it succeeds in expanding aggregate demand. If monetary policy is used and there is a world capital market that fixes the rate of interest for the country it will not be able to induce an expansion of investment demand, except in so far as the world rate of interest can be influenced. There may also be some cash-balance effect that increases consumption. But a budget deficit can normally still bring about a demand expansion, even if monetary policy alone does not succeed. In any case, the method of expansion—monetary or fiscal or some combination— is not central to the issue here. I shall just assume that there is a monetary or fiscal expansion.

Demand will then expand for non-traded goods, and this will achieve the desired reduction in unemployment. At the same time demand will expand for traded goods, and this will worsen the balance of payments. But the extra demand for non-traded goods will also raise their prices; this in turn will bring about a switching of the production pattern towards non-traded goods and of the demand pattern towards traded goods, and so worsen the balance of payments further. Even if the result were only to bring about a once-for-all deterioration of the balance of payments, there would be a running down of foreign-exchange reserves (or a continuous increase in the stock of foreign debts) that could not go on for ever. But if the rate of price change of non-traded goods rises to above 5 per cent (so that there is not just a once-for-all rise in their prices) there will be a continuously deteriorating balance of payments. The country's export and import-competing sectors would continuously decline in size. Thus this situation of a differential rate of inflation is certainly not a steady-state one. But it *can* go on for some time. There are, of course, monetary forces which tend to eliminate trade imbalances unless deliberately counteracted. Here we are assuming that such counteracting policies, in the form of continuous domestic-credit creation or a continuous budget deficit, are at work.

It is sometimes said that in a fixed-exchange-rate system a country cannot have an inflation rate that is different from the world rate. But this is too extreme a position. It is a position that can rest on either of two arguments.

First, it may be argued that the domestic prices of all goods are fixed in world markets by 'commodity arbitrage'. Unless tariffs are continuously raised, or domestic markets are separated from world markets by quotas or other controls, the prices of home-produced goods must go up at the same rate as the prices of the foreign goods with which they compete. But this assumes that all goods are traded goods, and ignores the large sector of non-traded goods and services, where prices are not closely tied to foreign prices. Because of product differentiation in manufacturing, even many so-called import-competing goods can show divergent price trends from prices of imports, although they will steadily lose competitiveness and sales if their prices are rising faster.

Secondly, the view that the rate of inflation cannot diverge from the world rate may rest on the balance-of-payments effects of such divergences. The implication is that the balance of payments cannot deteriorate for long, and that forces of rectification will soon set in. But it is possible to run down reserves or to borrow for long periods, and to sterilize the monetary forces of rectification.

The situation in the fixed-exchange-rate system is then that this particular inflation-prone country will have an inflation rate above 5 per cent for some time. It will run a balance-of-payments deficit, possibly an increasing one, and it will perhaps succeed in reducing unemployment, at least for a limited period. But this cannot go on for ever. Eventually it will have to change its policies and get back to a 5 per cent rate of inflation—and perhaps even for a time to a rate of less than 5 per cent in order to rebuild its foreign-exchange reserves.

The Story Continued: The Flexible Rate

Let us now imagine that the country is liberated from its commitment to a fixed rate. But let us replace it with another commitment, namely to desist from any deliberate intervention in the foreign-exchange market designed to affect the exchange rate. It will certainly now be *possible* for the country to have a permanently higher rate of inflation than the world rate. Monetary and fiscal policies would steadily expand domestic demand and so raise the prices of non-traded goods, and at the same time, continuous exchange-rate depreciation would raise the domestic prices of traded goods and so avoid any change in the price relationship between traded and non-traded goods.

We might then arrive at the following conclusion—which indeed has been often arrived at. We assume that the government of this particular country *wants* to attain a higher rate of inflation than the world rate for the sake of reducing unemployment. It wants to put the country on a point on the short-term Phillips curve that involves more than 5 per cent inflation and the lower unemployment that goes with this higher inflation rate. In the flexible-rate system the government will have no inhibitions in doing so. By contrast, in the fixed-rate system it can do so only at the cost of running down reserves, or foreign borrowing, or both—and this cannot go on for ever. Therefore, for *this* country the flexible-rate system is inflationary. The fixed-rate system imposed a balance-of-payments constraint that disappears once the exchange rate is allowed to alter.

Yet this is not the whole story. There is another argument, also popular, which one has to relate to the previous argument—even though the two arguments are not usually related.

In the fixed-rate system the country can export some of its inflation abroad. A given expansion of demand goes only partly on domestically produced goods and services. Partly it goes on foreign goods, or causes exports to fall, and so leads to a balance-of-payments deficit. This deficit means that the spending goes abroad, and so diverts part of the inflationary impact away from domestic goods and services. The argument can also be put in monetary terms. In the fixed-rate system domestic-credit creation increases the world money supply; the extra supply of money goes at least partly abroad and so has an inflationary impact there. By contrast, in the flexible-rate system the whole of the extra demand goes on domestically produced goods and services, and inflation is not exported. The country is not able to modify the inflationary impact of a monetary or fiscal expansion by absorbing more foreign goods and exporting less.

We could think of the process as a two-stage one, first holding the exchange rate constant and then allowing it to vary. The monetary or fiscal expansion initially worsens the balance of payments and creates modest inflation at home. Then the exchange rate depreciates, which eliminates the balance of payments deficit and increases the inflation at home. From a domestic point of view the depreciation is then inflationary.

The conclusion from this argument is that for a given domestic-demand expansion, the impact is certainly more inflationary at home when the exchange rate is flexible. If the monetary authorities were only concerned with the adverse effects of inflation, they would choose to have a lower demand expansion when the whole impact is felt at home than when some of it was exported. Combining this with our earlier argument, in the fixed-rate system the authorities are constrained by the adverse balance-of-payments effects of a monetary expansion, and in the flexible-rate system they are constrained by the greater domestic inflationary impact. A given monetary or fiscal expansion will certainly be more inflationary at home with a flexible-rate system, but one cannot take this monetary expansion as given. The monetary expansion may well be less in the flexible-rate system.

Where then does that leave us?

A More Systematic Approach

Let me now proceed to a more systematic approach which is meant to show how the various arguments given above fit together.

A given monetary or fiscal expansion has two distinct effects in the fixed-rate system. Firstly, it increases demand for domestic goods and services, and so increases employment and generates domestic inflation. One can suppose that there is a short-term Phillips curve which the monetary authorities have in mind, and that from this point of view there is an optimal point on that curve. Let us say that the optimal combination they prefer is 2 per cent unemployment and 7 per cent inflation. I am not saying that they are correct in their choice or that the curve is stable. If the monetary expansion brings the economy closer to that point, then it raises social welfare, at least as perceived by the authorities. The second effect of the monetary expansion is that it worsens the balance of payments. This effect leads to the absorption of extra resources by the economy in excess of domestic production, the cost of these resources being the rate of interest foregone on foreign-exchange reserves, the rate of interest paid on funds borrowed abroad, and the interest equivalent of the loss of security resulting from lower reserves. If borrowing involves some political commitments or losses of freedom there may also be political costs. This second effect does not arise in the flexible-rate system. It is a by-product of monetary and fiscal expansion designed to increase employment in the fixed-rate system. But, as I shall show, it may conceivably also be a reason for such expansion.

It is central to the systematic approach I am suggesting that one has to form a view about the welfare implications of this balance-of-payments deficit. On the one hand, there is a favourable effect: the economy absorbs more foreign resources. Extra demand is satisfied by foreign goods, or by reducing exports, and so involves no current sacrifice. The demand is diverted away from domestic goods, so that inflation—or some part of it—is 'exported'. But there is also an unfavourable aspect. The resources are obtained at a cost, which may be broadly expressed as a rate of interest. When the rate of interest becomes infinite, or at least very high, we can say that there is a balance-of-payments 'constraint'—no more funds can be obtained at reasonable cost. This is the aspect which is stressed in the earlier argument described above. Now we must combine these two aspects.

The simplest approach is the following. Let us assume that there is 'autonomous' borrowing abroad, private and public, which has brought the rate of foreign borrowing up to the point where, in the perception of the public decision-makers, the marginal social return is equal to the rate of interest payable. In that case any extra borrowing would inflict a loss. Now monetary and fiscal policy designed to stimulate the domestic economy will, as a by-product, generate such extra borrowing. It will worsen the balance of payments and give rise to 'accommodating borrowing' (or an accommodating decrease in lending in the form of a decline in foreign-exchange reserves). Given the assumption about the optimality of autonomous borrowing, this extra borrowing (or decrease in lending) will then inflict a social loss. The marginal gain in terms of the value of the extra resources obtained will fall below the rate of interest paid or foregone, as well as any non-pecuniary costs of borrowing.

This means that the unfavourable aspect of the balance-of-payments effect will outweigh the favourable aspect. Given this result, we have the following conclusion.

The desired rate of domestic-price inflation, at least in the short run, is 7 per cent. This is the inflation rate associated with the optimal point on the short-run perceived Phillips curve. In the flexible-rate system the monetary and fiscal expansion will be such as to attain this desired rate. In the fixed-rate system, by contrast, a monetary and fiscal expansion that leads to a domestic inflation rate of more than 5 per cent (the world rate) will create a growing balance-of-payments deficit, and this will inflict a net cost, the by-product cost of trying to get closer to the desired inflation rate. The monetary authorities will then find it optimal to trade off the gains of getting closer to the desired rate (7 per cent) against the costs of getting further away from the world rate (5 per cent), so perhaps ending up at 6 per cent. The costs of getting above the world rate—that is, the cost of running a balance-of-payments deficit—will steadily increase because the rate of interest payable will go up as the country's foreign assets decline or liabilities increase, and because the marginal product of the extra resources falls. Hence the optimal trade-off rate will steadily fall, approaching the world rate of 5 per cent, at which point the balance-of-payments deficit disappears.

We can thus sum up as follows for this 'inflation-prone' country. It has a desired rate of inflation greater than the world rate. In the flexible rate system its actual rate will be equal to that desired rate. By contrast, in the fixed-rate system its actual rate will initially be above the world rate, but *below* the desired rate, and will gradually move down to the world rate. Thus, if one means by 'rate of inflation', the rate of *price* inflation, the flexible-rate system for this country is more inflationary than the fixed-rate system.

This does not tell us whether the rate of monetary or fiscal expansion—that is, the rate of increase in the nominal level of absorption—will be greater in one system than in the other. On the one hand, it will tend to be higher in the flexible-rate system because the rate of price inflation will be higher. On the other hand, in the fixed-rate system monetary expansion also feeds the balance-of-payments deficit. If the nominal balance-of-payments deficit in the fixed-rate system increases at a faster rate than the domestic rate of price inflation would in the flexible system, then it is at least possible that the total rate of monetary expansion is greater under fixed rates. But one can say something a little less agnostic. As the balance-of-payments deficit will eventually have to fall and then disappear, eventually the rate of monetary expansion under the fixed-rate system will have to be lower than in the flexible-rate system, just as the rate of price increase will be lower.

Must there be a Loss from Accommodating Borrowing?

Before leaving this case of an inflation-prone country I should like to go back to the original argument that there must be a net loss from 'accommodating borrowing'. It was this argument that gave us a neat answer to what otherwise seemed a somewhat complicated problem. The key assumption was that 'autonomous' borrowing of the right amount was already taking place, and that the only reason for additional monetary or fiscal expansion was to increase domestic employment. Hence the objective of the monetary or fiscal expansion was *not* to transfer foreign resources to the public sector, even though such a transfer was an undesired by-product. In general, this approach seems the right one, though it may suggest a solution to our problem by a semantic trick: in so far as there is a net gain from foreign borrowing or running down reserves, it is defined as 'autonomous'; in so far as there is a net loss it is 'accommodating'.

A better and more orthodox approach is to define 'accommodating' borrowing or decrease in lending as that borrowing or decrease in lending that would not have taken place under the flexible-rate system. Accommodating borrowing must surely be defined as that borrowing which is the result of trying to maintain an exchange-rate commitment, and in the flexible-rate system there is no such commitment. Any borrowing under the flexible-rate system must be regarded as being motivated by a direct expectation of gain (leaving aside temporary interventions for exchange-rate-smoothing purposes).

It is at least conceivable that there is some gain at the margin from accommodating borrowing or decrease in lending. In that case, the rate of price inflation that the authorities would regard as optimal in the fixed-rate system would actually be higher than in the flexible-rate system. In other words, they would accept or create a domestic rate of price inflation above their desired rate for the sake of the by-product of borrowing cheaply abroad.

This case is not as implausible as it might seem, especially for a less-developed country. In the normal way a country may find it difficult to borrow other than at a high rate of interest. But it may be able to obtain low-interest emergency loans in a balance-of-payments crisis. In other words, accommodating borrowing may be cheaper than autonomous borrowing. Of course, there may be extra political costs in the emergency loans, and a country cannot have too many balance-of-payments crises yielding emergency loans, but it is not inconceivable that a country will follow somewhat more inflationary policies than otherwise for the sake of the real benefits to be derived from these loans.

The Inflation-Shy Country

So far I have been talking entirely of an 'inflation-prone' country—a country like Britain—which would achieve an inflation rate greater than the world rate if it were a free agent. In the flexible-rate system it *is* a free agent, while in the fixed-rate system it is not. The argument has been that in that case it is likely to choose an inflation rate somewhere between the world rate and the rate it really desires, this trade-off choice gradually moving down to the world rate. Of course, normally the government or monetary authorities would desire not an inflation rate as such but rather a level of employment that its authorities believe goes with the 'desired rate'; though it is also conceivable that the particular inflation rate is desired for its redistributive rather than its supposed employment-generating effects.

The whole analysis can be applied to an 'inflation-shy' country—a country like Germany which would choose an inflation rate less than the world rate if it were a free agent. In terms of short-term Phillips curve analysis this country may be inflation-shy either because it has a more favourable Phillips curve, so that it needs less inflation to get the rate of unemployment down to a desired level, or because it has social preferences which are more biased against inflation and less concerned about short-run unemployment. It is also possible that its authorities are less favourably inclined to the redistributive effects of inflation, compared to those of the inflation-prone country.

One can make the analysis quite symmetrical with that applying to the inflation-prone country.

In the fixed-rate system the inflation-shy country can—if it wants to—attain for some time a rate of inflation less than the world rate. This means that it would be running a continuously increasing balance-of-payments surplus, with a continuously expanding traded-goods sector, and continuous accumulation of foreign-exchange reserves. While the prices of traded goods would rise at the rate of world inflation, a tight demand policy would ensure that the prices of non-traded goods rose at a slower rate, so that the rate of increase of the average domestic price-level would fall below the world rate. But this would mean a continuous relative-price change, with resources moving out of non-traded into traded goods and demand shifting towards non-traded goods. Absorption would have to fall more and more below aggregate output. Aggregate output itself may of course be growing rapidly, as in the case of Germany for many years, so that, on balance, real absorption may also be growing. There will be a floor to the rate of increase of the average domestic price-level for any given rate of world inflation because the prices of non-traded goods are unlikely to fall absolutely however much demand expansion is held back.

But this asymmetry will be ignored for the moment and returned to in the next chapter.

The main point at this stage is that this country will have a desired inflation rate, say 2 per cent, which it will attain in the flexible-rate system. If it followed a fiscal and monetary policy that gave it this rate of inflation in the fixed-rate system—where the world rate of inflation is 5 per cent—it would find itself accumulating reserves and lending abroad in an accommodating fashion. It will give up resources to foreigners in return for receiving interest payments as well as a comforting sense of security. But, applying our earlier argument, we might assume that it incurs a net loss from this accommodating lending. The goods and services given up to foreigners are not sufficiently compensated for by the interest payments received and any non-pecuniary benefits. And this loss will increase as the surplus goes on. So the chosen inflation rate in the fixed-rate system (say 3 per cent) will be more than the desired rate (2 per cent) and will gradually move up towards the world rate (5 per cent).

The argument then is that a country like Germany will *choose* not to insulate herself completely from world inflation in the fixed-rate system. But for a time she will insulate herself partially. The assumption is that she *could* insulate herself; insulation is a matter of choice, not of technical possibilities. She cannot insulate herself from the rises in the prices of traded goods imposed by the world market, but the argument is that a tight demand policy can allow her to keep down the prices of non-traded goods—though at the cost of steady expansion of the traded goods sector and a continuous increase in the balance-of-payments surplus.

I am thus assuming that monetary sterilization is possible. It might be said that the domestic money supply *must* increase when the foreign assets of the banking system are increased by the accumulation of foreign-exchange reserves. But here one must remember that the domestic assets of the banking system can be decreased, or increased less. Nevertheless there may be some technical or practical limits here, so that some transmission of inflation through the monetary mechanism is perhaps inevitable.

In that case one might sum up the transmission process in the fixed-rate system as follows. First, there is some automatic transmission through the prices of traded goods rising with world inflation. This is so-called 'commodity arbitrage'. Secondly, there is some automatic transmission through the money supply having to increase to a minimum extent and so pushing up demand for non-traded goods. But it is the third element of the process on which I am focusing in this chapter. There may be some deliberate further increase in the money supply or fiscal expansion, this time not automatic but the result of an optimizing policy, designed to reduce and eventually eliminate the balance-of-payments surplus that would otherwise result.

Conclusion so far

After all this, I have arrived at a well-known conclusion. In the flexible-rate system each country can choose whatever inflation rate it wishes. The inflation-prone country—Britain—chooses a high rate, while the inflation-shy country—Germany—chooses a low rate. Exchange-rate flexibility insulates these countries with their different inflation tastes from each other. It is the system of flexible rates which in 1974 allowed an 8 per cent inflation rate in Germany to coexist with a 26 per cent rate in Britain. The prices of traded goods tend to be equalized when converted at the variable exchange rate. In sterling terms they are rising much faster than in terms of D-marks. By contrast, in the fixed-rate system each country's inflation rate will be drawn towards some average world rate. While the inflation rates will not be necessarily equalized, they will *tend* towards equality. Britain is still likely to have a higher rate than Germany for long periods, but the divergence will be much less than in the flexible-rate system, and will get less over time (in the absence of structural changes and shocks of various kinds).

Thus one cannot say that for the world as a whole the fixed-rate system is more or less inflationary than the flexible-rate one. For Britain the fixed-rate system is less inflationary, and for Germany more. In the case of Britain the fixed-rate system forces her to restrain her monetary expansion because of what is usually called the balance of payments constraint—which is better described as the net cost of running a deficit. In the case of Germany the fixed-rate system forces Germany to be more inflationary than otherwise because of the relatively unrewarding surplus she is building up—a surplus which has meant that she is giving up goods for the use of foreigners with relatively little reward in interest payments.

A World of Reluctant Exchange-Rate Adjustment

The so-called fixed-exchange-rate world up to August 1971 (and again, from the Smithsonian agreement of December 1971 until March 1973) was not really a world of firmly fixed exchange rates. Rather, it was a world of reluctant exchange-rate adjustments. Many countries depreciated their currencies—some, like France, with less reluctance than others. Some countries also appreciated their currencies, though this was certainly less common than depreciation. But neither of our two extreme models correctly represents this world. Similarly, one could argue that the world since March 1973 has not been a world of true exchange-rate flexibility where countries have felt uninhibited about exchange-rate alterations. Some countries have still felt somewhat inhibited, and intermittently have tried to fix their rates. It follows that one really needs a model for an intermediate world.

There is, in fact, a continuum. At one end is the world of firmly fixed rates. At the other end is a world where monetary authorities feel no commitment at all to particular exchange rates. What has happened is that the O.E.C.D. countries have moved quite sharply in the direction of this latter world. They feel much less commitment to particular exchange rates and are thus much less reluctant either to make discrete alterations or to allow the market to make the alterations for them. Of course, some developing countries, notably in Latin America, never showed much reluctance even before 1971.

Let us assume that a country sees a benefit in having its exchange rate fixed. There is then a cost from any exchange-rate alteration, whether up or down. We can think of this as a political cost or alternatively as an economic cost concerned with the inconvenience for trade and capital movements of variable exchange rates. Because of this cost, any exchange-rate adjustment will be reluctant. The political cost could result essentially from the domestic income redistribution between the traded and the non-traded goods sectors that is brought about by a significant exchange-rate alteration. This political cost may arise even though the exchange-rate adjustment only reverses the redistributive effects of a difference between the domestic and the world-inflation rates. The economic cost may be much the same for a large as for a small exchange-rate alteration, so that it will generally be optimal to make discrete rather than continuous adjustments.

If the country's inflation rate diverges from the world rate and the exchange rate is fixed, the country will, on the basis of our earlier analysis, run a balance-of-payments imbalance and so incur a cost. Our analysis so far has suggested that it will reduce this cost by bringing its inflation rate somewhat away from its 'desired' rate, but closer—though not equal to—the world rate. Now we must allow for the alternative policy of altering the exchange rate. I do not assume that the exchange-rate alteration is so automatic and large that any balance-of-payments imbalance is completely avoided. Rather, exchange-rate alteration is introduced as an additional policy option in a world of essentially pegged rates.

The elements of the cost-benefit calculus are then as follows. Running the payments imbalance imposes a cost. Altering the exchange rate also imposes a cost. As the cost of payments imbalance increases—and it will increase as the foreign-exchange reserves run down or up, or as foreign indebtedness rises—it will become optimal to make a discrete exchange-rate adjustment. Thus we are now in a world where there are both costs from payments imbalances—that is, from accommodating capital movements—and costs from discrete exchange-rate adjustments. There are two types of costs and monetary authorities will balance these against each other.

The important question is how inflation rates will be affected by the availability in the short term of two ways of making different inflation rates between countries compatible. The answer is that qualitatively the conclusions of our fixed-exchange rate model still apply. If a country's inflation rate diverges from the world rate, an inevitable cost will be incurred. This cost will be some mix of the cost of accommodating capital movements and the cost of exchange-rate alteration. Monetary authorities will then trade off this combined cost against the benefits from getting the domestic inflation rates (and short-term levels of employment) they want. They would then modify their monetary and fiscal policies so as to bring their inflation rates somewhat away from their 'desired' rates closer towards the world rate.

While the conclusion is qualitatively the same, quantitatively it may be different if exchange-rate alteration is not seen as having very large costs. When the possibility of exchange-rate adjustment is introduced, the cost to the country of any given divergence of its own inflation rate from the world rate is reduced. The country will thus choose an inflation rate in this system which is closer to its desired rate than the inflation rate it would have chosen in a situation where the exchange rate was absolutely unalterable.

One could generalize as follows. The greater the perceived costs of exchange-rate adjustment, whether political or economic, the closer the results of this intermediate model are to the results of the fixed-exchange-rate model. The less these exchange-rate adjustments cost, the closer the results to those of the flexible-rate model. The flexible-rate model represents the limiting case where no costs of exchange-rate adjustment are perceived at all.

How is the World Rate of Inflation Determined in the Fixed-rate System?

Let me now return to the system where exchange rates are completely fixed. One has to explain how the world rate of inflation— the average of inflation rates in different countries—is determined in that system. I have not worked this out fully, though I am sure it could be done, especially if one simplified it to a two-country model. Given the inflation rates in other countries, each country has an optimal inflation rate, with an associated deficit (if its optimal rate is above the world rate) or surplus (if its optimal rate is below the world rate). The real interest rate is a variable in this model. If many countries want to inflate at a high rate and run deficits, this will raise the real rate of interest and discourage deficit and encourage surplus countries—in other words, bring down the world-inflation rate. If one country's desire to inflate rises, so that its inflation rate is increased, it will pull up all the other countries' inflation rates, since their optimal rates rise when their neighbours' actual inflation rates go up. A large trading economy, or one willing to run big imbalances, will have a bigger effect on other countries' optimal rates than smaller economies. Hence, when the United States chooses to become more inflationary this will have a significant effect on the inflation rates of other countries.

Let me conclude then by referring to the popular issue of the 'export of inflation' by the United States. It has been a common European view that, in the fixed-rate system which operated until August 1971, the United States 'exported' her inflation. There was possibly an automatic element in this 'export' of inflation through the rise in the prices of traded goods. And there may also have been some element of monetary transmission that would have been difficult to avoid even if non-U.S. monetary authorities had wanted to—and had reacted with speed and foresight to developments. But another possible interpretation is that countries found themselves accumulating dollars and so foregoing the use of resources at home for the benefit of the United States ('financing the Vietnam War', as unfriendly critics used to say). At the same time, they did not find the interest receipts on their dollars and the sense of security they got from, at least, the last lot of dollars, sufficiently rewarding. Hence—explicitly or implicitly—they chose to inflate away some of their surpluses and keep the so-called 'dollar flood' in check.

There is certainly more to this issue, and I shall come back to it in Chapter 6. It has to be remembered that it was only in 1970 that official reserves of dollars increased significantly, for until then the dollars tended to go into private holdings. Furthermore, as I have just pointed out, it has to be remembered that the system was not one of rigidly fixed exchange rates. Countries were free to appreciate their exchange rates. If they did not do so sufficiently, and chose to allow domestic inflation instead, this was also a choice. But the argument presented here may have some validity in so far as countries felt, for one reason or another, some constraint on their exchange-rate policies.

INFLATION UNDER FIXED
AND FLEXIBLE RATES

In Figure 2 the vertical axis shows an index of social welfare as perceived by the government and/or central bank of a particular country. The horizontal axis shows the country's rate of price inflation. The curve w w' shows how perceived welfare varies with the short-run rate of inflation. With each rate of inflation is associated a particular level of short-run unemployment as well as expectations about long-run unemployment and about future rates of inflation. Also, there are associated income-distribution effects. The curve w w' takes the expected employment and income-distribution effects into account.

If the country is subject to a flexible-exchange-rate regime it chooses the optimal point A, with inflation rate os. This is the 'desired' inflation rate.

Now consider the fixed-rate regime. Assume that the given world rate of inflation is o R. Let there be no structural changes, no autonomous capital movements, and no shifts in demand patterns or differences in productivity growth that might make differences in rates of inflation compatible with an unchanged balance of payments. The balance of

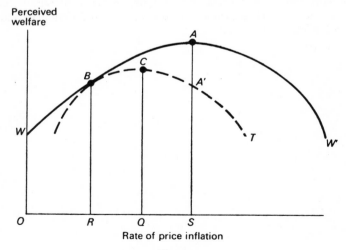

FIG. 2

payments will then be in equilibrium (i.e. no accommodating capital movements) if the country's inflation rate is also OR.

If the inflation rate exceeded OR in a given time-period, the country would run a deficit. Assuming that this yields a net welfare loss (interest payments etc. exceed value of extra resources obtained) the perceived welfare curve becomes BT. For example, at inflation rate OS, the loss from the deficit in the relevant period is AA'.

The optimal point on BT is C, and the inflation rate becomes OQ. It is greater than the world rate OR but less than the 'desired' rate OS. As time goes on, and foreign-exchange reserves decline, or accumulated accommodating debts build up, the curve BT swings down tending to become vertical. So C moves to the left, towards B, and eventually the chosen inflation rate will have to be OR.

In Figure 2 the country is an inflation-prone country, since the desired inflation rate exceeds the given world rate. In the case of an inflation-*shy* country, the point B would be to the right of A, the desired rate being lower than the world rate. The inflation rate in the fixed rate system—OQ—would then be higher than that in the flexible-rate system.

Furthermore, in Figure 2 there is a net welfare *loss* from accommodating borrowing, or running down of reserves. If there were a net gain, BT would run *above* BW'. Assuming continuity, C would be to the right of A, so that the inflation-prone country would initially choose a higher rate of inflation under the fixed-rate regime than under the flexible-rate regime.

If inflation in the rest of the world increased, so that B moved to the right, it would cause the chosen point under the fixed regime, C, to move to the right. Hence the rest of the world would have exported its rise in inflation to this country.

REFERENCES

A theoretical paper on the subject is Joel Fried, 'Inflation–Unemployment Trade-offs under Fixed and Floating Exchange Rates,' *Canadian Journal of Economics*, 6 (February 1973), 43–52. Wide-ranging discussions of the world inflation–exchange rate issues are in G. Haberler, 'Inflation as a World-wide Phenomenon', *Weltwirtschaftliches Archiv*, 110, No. 2 (1974), 179–93, and Harry G. Johnson, 'World Inflation and the International Monetary System', *The Three Banks Review* (September 1973), 3–22. The chapter is a development and fuller exposition of W. M. Corden, 'Inflation and the Exchange Rate Regime', *Scandinavian Journal of Economics*, 78 (1976), 370–83.

There are quite a number of papers discussing the extent to which countries have actually sterilized monetary inflows. One of these papers is Victor Argy and Pentti J. K. Kouri, 'Sterilization Policies and Volatility in International Reserves', in R. Z. Aliber (ed.), *National Monetary Policies and the International Financial System*, University of Chicago Press, 1974, and indeed many of the papers in this book are relevant to the issues in this and other chapters here.

In addition, see R. J. Herring and R. C. Marston, *National Monetary Policies and International Financial Markets*, North-Holland, Amsterdam, 1977, where the theory of sterilization is clearly set out. This book shows how the effects of sterilization and of offsetting capital flows in a world of significant but imperfect capital mobility are related. From a careful study of the German case in the sixties and early seventies the authors conclude that the Bundesbank sterilized balance of payments flows almost completely.

5

INFLATION AND THE EXCHANGE-RATE SYSTEM: SOME ASYMMETRIES

I N the previous chapter the analysis was completely symmetrical. It was impossible to conclude that for the world as a whole the flexible-rate system has an inflationary or deflationary bias. One could say only that the system gives governments freedom—the freedom to follow inflationary or deflationary policies as they wish. In their choices they need not be influenced by the choices of other governments. By contrast, in the fixed-rate system governments influence each other. While they would still have some freedom in their macro-economic policies in the short run, the choice of one government with regard to macro-economic policy would be influenced by the choices of other governments. The tendency would be for all the inflation rates to come together. In this system the influence on the policies of other countries of a large trading and investing economy—notably the United States—would be particularly great.

In this chapter and the next I want to look at some possible asymmetries. These provide the bases for common assertions that —in spite of the symmetrical arguments of the previous chapter— one can generalize about which exchange-rate regime is more inflationary for the world as a whole.

There are really just two asymmetries to consider. The first is the tendency for money wages and hence prices to be flexible upwards, but to be rigid—or at least less flexible—downwards. Three separate arguments or aspects have to be looked at here, all of them resting on this general type of asymmetry. I begin in this chapter with an examination of these three arguments. The second asymmetry concerns the special case of the reserve-currency country, to which I shall come in the next chapter.

Can the Inflation-Shy Country Insulate Itself from World Inflation?

It was a central theme of the previous lecture that an inflation-shy country such as Germany *could*, if it wished, have an inflation rate lower than the world rate even in the fixed-rate system. But it was argued that there were costs to Germany of such a divergence from the world inflation rate, so it would *choose* gradually to bring its inflation rate up to the world rate.

This argument has now to be modified in the following way. In the fixed-rate regime there is a lower limit to the inflation rate that Germany can attain, given the world inflation rate. If the prices of non-traded goods are determined by wage-costs (there being, perhaps, a constant percentage profit-mark-up in the non-traded sector), and if money wages are rigid downwards, then prices of non-traded goods and services cannot fall. The lower limit to the general rate of price increase in Germany is then set by the weighted average of the world inflation rate—which determines the rate at which domestic prices of traded goods rise in Germany —and the zero rate of the non-traded sector. This assumes that no limit is set by any difficulties in sterilizing the monetary effects of the growing balance-of-payments surplus. If the size of the non-traded sector is small there is then really rather little scope for Germany's inflation rate to diverge from the world rate. One should add that it will become smaller as a result of Germany's inflation rate being held below other countries' because its profitability will steadily fall relative to that of the traded-goods sector.

The point would be important if Germany's desired inflation rate were zero or very low—and if the size of the non-traded sector were very small. With the world inflation rate positive, a German rate of zero could not be attained in the fixed-rate system since it would require the prices of non-traded goods actually to fall. There are two qualifications to this argument. Firstly, in the last few years the desired rates even in the inflation-shy countries have been well above zero, so that this constraint has hardly arisen. This does not mean, of course, that governments in such countries as Germany, Switzerland, and the Netherlands have actually 'desired' inflation rates that were very high by their own standards; rather, they have not desired the short-run unemployment that would go with lower inflation rates. The second qualification is that prices of non-traded goods could decline somewhat, even when money wages are rigid downwards, through the squeezing of profit margins in the non-traded sector.

It must also be added that this general issue is, in any case, not very important to our central theme. It says only that in the fixed-rate system Germany would not be able to keep her inflation rate far below the world rate, at least when the world rate is not very high. But our main point has been that, in any case, Germany will not *want* to keep her inflation rate below the world rate for any length of time, because she will not want to have a growing balance-of-payments surplus. Hence this particular point is only a small wrinkle in our main argument.

The Asymmetry of Surplus and Deficit Countries

Another, more important, argument runs as follows. It has been put by Gottfried Haberler, so I shall call it the 'Haberler' argument.

In the fixed-rate system surplus countries restore equilibrium by allowing their domestic prices to rise. On the other hand, deficit countries cannot get their domestic prices to fall because of the downward rigidity of money wages. Their contribution to the restoration of balance-of-payments equilibrium can only be to create domestic unemployment. Normally both surplus and deficit countries will want to make some contribution to the restoration of balance because of the costs of imbalances to both of them. The higher the foreign-exchange reserves of the deficit countries and the more international liquidity there is, the more of the contribution will have to come from the surplus countries, and hence the more inflationary the final result. It follows then that the fixed-rate system has an inflationary bias—with prices rising in surplus countries and not falling in deficit countries—while the flexibility of exchange rates eliminates this asymmetry, and so is less inflationary.

The main qualification is that this argument is hardly relevant in a world where all countries are inflating, the deficit countries just being the countries that are inflating rather more. Of course, a country may have become a deficit country because of structural shifts against it, or because of capital movements, and so it need not be a high-inflation country to start with. But as long as its inflation rate is significantly positive, it can make its contribution to the restoration of equilibrium by lowering its inflation rate. It does not actually need to bring about a negative inflation rate.

When all countries are inflating, there need be no asymmetry at all. The surplus countries will just inflate somewhat more in order to make their contribution to the restoration of balance, while the deficit countries inflate somewhat less. There would then be an asymmetry only if it were generally easier to raise than to lower the inflation *rate*. The argument was developed in the sixties, at a time when there was concern about world inflation, but when the average world inflation rate was still quite low.

The Adverse Asymmetrical Effects of Exchange-Rate Fluctuations

I come now to an argument that has apparently originated with Robert Mundell and Arthur Laffer, but that at first sight seems to be diametrically opposed to the previous one. One will immediately be faced with the question of reconciling the two arguments.

A floating exchange rate leads to big fluctuations in exchange rates induced in the main by capital movements. Changing expectations and divergent interest rate policies cause portfolio preferences of asset-holders to change—one month asset-holders move *en masse* into D-marks, the next into dollars, and so on. These exchange-rate fluctuations then cause asymmetrical price reactions. When the Swiss franc appreciates, Swiss domestic prices of traded goods fail to go down, because of the usual downward rigidity of money wages. Rather, the appreciation leads to unemployment. On the other hand, when the Swiss franc subsequently depreciates, Swiss prices of traded goods certainly go up, perhaps followed in due course to some extent by prices of non-traded goods. The argument is that price fluctuations brought about by exchange-rate fluctuations have 'ratchet effects' with a net inflationary result.

The most important single exchange-rate relationship is now the dollar–D-mark rate. There have certainly been marked fluctuations in this rate in the 1973–5 period. Thus in January 1974 the dollar was 20 per cent above its rate six months earlier, then it dropped 15 per cent in the next four months and later in the year it dropped another 15 per cent, but then in 1975 it rose again at least 10 per cent. This must have led to fluctuations in the price-levels of some traded goods in Germany—and perhaps also in the United States—much more than any fluctuations in the general price-level.

This Mundell–Laffer argument is subject to the same important qualification as the Haberler argument. These asymmetries are unlikely to arise when price-levels in the relevant countries are all rising at a fast rate in any case. An appreciation of the D-mark will then simply modify the rate of inflation of traded goods prices in Germany; it need not cause unemployment or bring the inflation rate of traded goods prices to zero. Appreciation *will* then cause prices to rise more slowly just as depreciation caused them to rise faster, so that the reaction is symmetrical. But let us look at the argument further, assuming that there is an asymmetry and hence a ratchet effect because of the large size of the exchange-rate fluctuations in a context where inflation rates of appreciating countries are *not* high.

The question is whether this problem would also arise in a fixed-rate system. If the exchange rates were utterly, unalterably, fixed there would be no capital movements speculating on future exchange rates. But the relevant comparison is with the Bretton Woods system where the rates were alterable and often expected to alter, so that there were indeed vast speculative capital movements. In addition, in the fixed-rate system, as in the flexible-rate system, there will be fluctuations in capital movements derived from changes in assessments of underlying profitability conditions in different countries. The question then is how such fluctuations in capital movements, however caused, are coped with in the fixed-rate system. If their domestic monetary impact were neutralized there would be no ratchet effects. On the other hand, if they were dealt with by the usual equilibrating methods—surplus countries inflating and deficit countries deflating—we would get exactly the same ratchet effects: prices in surplus countries would rise, but prices in deficit countries would not fall. In fact, this is the Haberler argument.

The central issue really is this. Let us take as given certain fluctuations in private capital movements which can, for the present purpose, be treated as exogenous. If countries do not offset these fluctuations externally and internally, then the current account will have to be adjusted to transfer the capital movements. The adjustment of the current account can be brought about either by exchange-rate alterations that change prices of traded goods (and perhaps indirectly of non-traded goods); or it can be brought about by changes in prices of non-traded goods resulting from equilibrating fiscal and monetary policies. As there must be relative and absolute price-level changes in both cases, there can in both cases be ratchet effects. It follows then that the Haberler argument and the Mundell–Laffer argument seem to be two sides of the same coin. Haberler focuses on the ratchet effect in the fixed-rate system, and Mundell–Laffer on the same phenomenon in the flexible-rate system.

If this ratchet effect is to be avoided, then the fluctuations in private-capital movements must be offset by changes in reserves or official borrowing or lending. In the fixed-rate system domestic price-level and employment changes can then be avoided, so that prices need not rise in the surplus country and employment does not need to fall in the deficit country. In the flexible-rate system there must then be *managed* floating—so that domestic prices of the deficit country need not rise (owing to depreciation) nor need employment fall in the surplus country (owing to appreciation). The only difference between the fixed- and the flexible-rate system is that in the fixed-rate system, current account adjustment is inflationary for the surplus country and deflationary for the deficit country, while in the flexible-rate system it is the other way around. Ratchet effects are created in both cases by the need for current-account adjustment. If this adjustment is avoided, the possibility of ratchet effects also disappears.

The general conclusion then is that a non-intervention system is likely to be more inflationary than a *rational* intervention system. I define the latter as management of the monetary base and of official borrowing and lending so as to offset fluctuations in the private capital account. Indeed, there could also be autonomous fluctuations in the current account (perhaps owing to changes in the terms of trade) that give rise to the need for such intervention. One has to emphasize the need for the intervention to be rational or stabilizing, since clearly intervention could increase fluctuations or even generate instabilities that would be entirely absent without intervention—as it may have done in countries such as the U.K. From this point of view, free floating may indeed be more inflationary than rationally managed floating. But for all the reasons given in the previous chapter, it does not follow that a system of flexible rates—whether managed or free floating—is necessarily more or less inflationary than a fixed-rate system.

Why have there been more Devaluations than Appreciations?

So far I have looked at asymmetries in the fixed-rate system and in the floating-rate system. Let us now turn to the real world where the intermediate model of reluctant exchange-rate adjustment is the relevant one. One can observe that in the post-war period up to August 1971 there were many more devaluations than appreciations. Thus there was an asymmetrical response to payments imbalances. The question is whether this is a new sort of asymmetry, one which I have not yet considered in this chapter, or whether it is a manifestation of the basic asymmetry discussed so far. Furthermore, what are the implications of this asymmetrical exchange-rate response for world inflation rates?

There are two possible explanations for this asymmetrical or biased response. Firstly, it may be that deficit countries are forced to adjust before surplus countries, borrowing being harder than lending. I shall call this the *adjustment bias*. Secondly, it may be that cost-level (non-exchange rate) adjustment is easier for surplus than for deficit countries because of the downward rigidity of money wages. So surplus countries tend to adjust by inflating their domestic costs while deficit countries have to adjust through exchange-rate alteration. I shall call this the *wage-rigidity bias*. Combining these two explanations, one can summarize as follows. For a country that has a payments imbalance there are three options: financing, cost-level adjustment, and exchange-rate adjustment. The deficit country may be more likely to choose the last, compared with the surplus country, either because financing is relatively more difficult for it (adjustment bias) or because cost-level adjustment is more difficult (wage-rigidity bias).

Let me spell out these two possible explanations of the asymmetrical exchange-rate response a little further, beginning with the adjustment bias. In the symmetrical model expounded in the previous chapter both deficit and surplus countries had incentives to reduce payments imbalances. This rested on the assumption that both deficit and surplus countries incurred net losses from accommodating capital movements. But it is possible that the losses are much greater for deficit countries, or at least manifest themselves much earlier. Indeed once a deficit country runs out of foreign-exchange reserves it may find it impossible to borrow other than at severe political cost or exhorbitant interest rates, and possibly it may not be able to borrow at all. Thus deficit countries are forced to adjust before surplus countries. Germany can keep on building up her reserves with impunity, but eventually countries such as Britain or Italy must do something drastic about their deficits. This has been a familiar argument. Of course, it may not apply in this form to the reserve-currency country (and hence, at one time, not to Britain), but the reserve-currency country case I shall discuss in the next chapter.

The argument has been more familiar in deficit than in surplus countries. In surplus countries it has been correctly said that the more international liquidity there is, the longer deficit countries can postpone adjustment, and that this forces the initiative for adjustment onto surplus countries. This view can be interpreted as saying that the interest-rate return that surplus countries get on their accommodating lending is less than the social return they could get if these resources were used for domestic consumption or investment. It is then certainly in their interests that adjustment takes place, even though one can hardly say that they 'have to' adjust.

Thus it is at least possible that there is some asymmetry or bias in the adjustment response, deficit countries being often forced to act before surplus countries. While the final result, in real economic terms, might be no different when the deficit country depreciates rather than when the surplus country appreciates (each adjusting absorption appropriately at the same time), there may be a difference in political terms. The country that has to take the initiative may incur a domestic political cost. In any case, here is at least one possible reason why there have been more depreciations than appreciations. It rests on an asymmetry which I have not discussed so far.

The second possible explanation for the asymmetrical exchange-rate response is the wage-rigidity bias. It rests on the asymmetrical behaviour of money wages which has been the central theme of this chapter. For both surplus and deficit countries it is easier to raise prices and wages than to lower them. The surplus country has no difficulty at all inflating away its surplus, and this is what surplus countries—given time—usually do. A sufficient appreciation of its exchange rate, on the other hand, might lead to an absolute fall in the domestic prices of its traded goods, and in the short run this is very likely to lead to unemployment owing to the downward rigidity of money wages and some immobility of factors between sectors. Allowing the domestic wage and price-level to rise is clearly the easiest option because of this wage-rigidity bias. The exception to this is a country such as Germany where there is an exceptional historically based fear of inflation. But even in that case some degree of domestic inflation did turn out to be politically much easier for a long time than sufficient appreciation.

By contrast with the surplus country, the wage-rigidity bias causes the deficit country to find it much easier to raise the relative domestic prices of traded goods by depreciation, than by lowering the absolute price-level of its non-traded goods. Deflation alone would create short-term unemployment, so it has to be accompanied by depreciation.

Is the Asymmetrical Exchange-rate Response Inflationary or Deflationary?

Let us look again at the first explanation of the asymmetrical exchange-rate response, namely the adjustment bias. Suppose it were true that deficit countries, rather than surplus countries, have to take the initiative in adjusting. Would this be inflationary? Surplus countries can choose their own inflation rates and ignore the balance-of-payments consequences. Deficit countries then have the option of lowering their rates of inflation or depreciating, or some combination of the two. Let us think of this in terms of a small deficit country. The prices of traded goods in foreign currency and the rates of increase in these prices are given to it. It has the option either of following a deflationary policy which will slow up the rate of increase in the prices of its non-traded goods, or of devaluing, which will raise the domestic prices of its traded goods relative to what they would have been otherwise.

In other words, the need for adjustment by the deficit country means that the domestic-price ratio between traded and non-traded goods must change. When the deficit country makes the adjustment this means that either the prices of its non-traded goods must fall (relative to what they would have been in the absence of adjustment) or the domestic prices of its traded goods must rise. Thus one cannot say that the adjustment bias—the need for adjustment by the deficit country rather than the surplus country—has a net inflationary effect. Indeed, if the deficit country used *both* the method of exchange-rate adjustment and the method of downward pressure on the domestic price-level of its non-traded goods, its average price-level might not be affected by its adjustment policies at all.

Now, let us look at the second explanation of the asymmetrical exchange-rate response, the wage-rigidity bias. Surplus countries adjust by allowing their domestic costs to increase. Thus they bring about the necessary change in the relative prices of traded and non-traded goods by allowing the prices of their non-traded goods to rise. On the other hand, deficit countries cannot easily bring down the prices of their non-traded goods, and so adjust by depreciating. The prices of their non-traded goods stay constant, but the depreciation raises the domestic currency prices of their traded goods. Thus in both countries the average price-level rises. In the surplus country it rises because of what I called earlier the Haberler effect, and in the deficit country it rises essentially because of what I called the Mundell–Laffer effect.

In this case the source of the asymmetry is the asymmetrical behaviour of money wages; it is this that compels the surplus country to avoid appreciation and that prevents the deficit country from lowering the prices of its non-traded goods. The net result of this asymmetry is inflationary. If inflation for this reason is to be avoided, financing has to take the place of adjustment. Thus the conclusions which applied to the two extreme models of the fixed and the flexible-rate regime also apply to the intermediate regime of reluctant exchange-rate adjustment.

REFERENCES

The 'Haberler argument' is in G. Haberler, 'Inflation as a World-wide Phenomenon', *Weltwirtschaftliches Archiv*, 110, No. 2 (1974), 179–93. The so-called 'Mundell–Laffer' argument is outlined in Emil-Maria Claassen, 'World Inflation under Flexible Exchange Rates', *Scandinavian Journal of Economics*, 78 (1976), 356–50 (for this argument seems to have earlier appeared in print only in articles in the Wall Street Journal).

6

THE RESERVE-CURRENCY ROLE AND THE EXPORT OF INFLATION BY THE UNITED STATES

In this chapter I come to an issue which is central to all discussions of the recent world inflation. How did inflation spread from the United States? In what sense, if any, did she 'export' her inflation? And did other countries have to import it? If they did not have to, why did they choose to? All these questions could be answered by using the straightforward symmetrical model of Chapter 4. The fact that the United States was—and is—a reserve-currency country need hardly come into the story. But there are various arguments and models that give a central place to the reserve-currency role and I want to examine and sort these out. In particular, I want to ask whether the reserve-currency role is likely to have induced the United States to follow a more inflationary policy than she would have otherwise.

How the United States Exported Inflation: the Policy Reactions

The story which is by now conventional—at least in monetarist circles and perhaps beyond—is that the United States chose to run a large fiscal deficit to finance the Vietnam War. After a lag this generated both inflation within the United States and the 'dollar flood'. This, in turn, brought about inflation in other countries, notably Western Europe and Japan. The inflation-transmission mechanism went partly through a direct price effect (prices of traded goods rising because American prices rose and because exchange rates were generally fixed), partly through an automatic-liquidity mechanism (the dollars pouring in to foreign countries not being fully sterilized), and partly through deliberate policy reactions (balance-of-payments surpluses of foreign countries removed the balance of payments as a restraint on expansionary monetary and fiscal policies). Generally it has been implied in much of the literature that the transmission of inflation was, in some sense, automatic, and that governments could do little about it. The deliberate policy reactions are then either underplayed or seen as part of an *automatic* policy reaction.

This story has to be qualified, which I shall do shortly. First, let us accept the basic story and analyse it in terms of our fixed-exchange-rate model. In that case we emphasize the deliberate policy reactions of other countries. For the purpose we take the fixed-exchange rate as given. When the world's largest economy inflates, the first impact is to yield a large balance-of-payments surplus for other countries. Their desired inflation rates (the rates they would have chosen in a flexible rate system) do not alter. But they now find that they are incurring costs through the balance-of-payments surpluses they are earning. They are giving up real resources ('helping to finance the Vietnam War') but not getting an adequate rate of interest to compensate for this. So they inflate their economies to reduce the surpluses. In this way the policy reactions in these countries have caused the U.S. to 'export' inflation to them. They did not *have* to import the U.S. inflation. It was their choice. But the choice was optimal, and perhaps inevitable.

This approach assumes that the whole transmission of inflation was a policy choice. Alternatively, one could assume that there was some automatic transmission of inflation. A rise in traded goods prices was inevitable, and this could not be compensated by a fall in non-traded goods prices because of the downward rigidity of money wages. Furthermore, it was probably technically impossible in the short run to sterilize all inflows. One could then suppose that the actual transmission had an automatic and a policy component. First came the automatic transmission. Then the policy transmission was added, designed to bring the inflation rate to the 'trade-off' point. The extent of the automatic transmission would not affect the final result; it would only set a lower limit to the extent to which inflation was transmitted.

This is a simple way of combining the automatic and the policy transmission elements without really affecting the final result of our model. But it is not quite satisfactory. The extent of automatic transmission may actually affect the final result. One might suppose that the automatic transmission started off the acceleration of inflation in the foreign countries. This then set up inflationary expectations. These inflationary expectations in turn necessitated higher rates of actual inflation if full employment was to be maintained. Hence the desired inflation rates of foreign countries were raised. Therefore the final 'trade-off' inflation rates at which these countries implicitly aimed, and which they attained by deliberate policies and not just by automatic transmission of inflation, were increased. The higher the automatic transmission, the higher the inflation rates finally chosen.

Qualifications to a Simple Story

There are two qualifications to this simple picture. Firstly, the rate of price inflation in the United States during the relevant period was not markedly higher than that in the other major industrial countries, and indeed, in several cases it was clearly lower. One cannot really say, therefore, that the U.S. exported her price inflation and that the international transmission process spread from the U.S. through a direct-price effect. Rather, the U.S. monetary and fiscal expansion led *both* to some domestic price inflation in the U.S. *and*—through the liquidity mechanism and through the deliberate policy reactions of foreign monetary authorities—to price inflation in foreign countries. The U.S. exported a large part of the inflationary impact of her monetary and fiscal expansion because of the fixed exchange-rate system, and by exporting it she actually had less price inflation at home than otherwise.

The second qualification concerns the details of how the 'dollar flood' originated and how it ended up as officially held reserves in other countries. The story is quite intricate, and not as simple as was outlined earlier. There were large U.S. federal-budget deficits only in some years, namely 1968, 1971, and 1972 (in 1968 it was under 3 per cent of G.N.P. and in the other two years even less). The current account was in small deficit in 1968, 1969, and 1971, with the first significant deficit in 1972 (but still less than 1 per cent of G.N.P.).

The important point is that until 1970 U.S. liquid liabilities to foreign *official* authorities did not increase. The dollars that went abroad were held by *private* foreigners. In 1968 holdings by private foreigners increased 23 per cent and in 1969 they increased another 47 per cent. Then in 1970 and 1971 the low-interest-rate policy of the U.S. (in real terms), and uncertainty about the dollar exchange rate in relation to other exchange rates, led to a large shift out of dollars by private foreign holders, and these dollars were then taken up by foreign governments. The large increase in foreign official reserves in 1970 and the vast increase in 1971 (in the two years together these reserves more than trebled) was due much more to the reduction in the private demand for dollars than to current-account deficits or long-term capital outflow in those years. On the other hand, by 1972 the shift out of dollars by the private sector appears to have come to an end, and the increase in officially held dollars in that year was more or less equal to that year's U.S. current-account deficit.

Thus one cannot say that U.S. current-account deficits increased foreign reserves every year. Rather, in the 1960s the current-account deficits combined with outflow of long-term capital increased private holdings of U.S. dollars, and these private holdings moved into official reserves rather suddenly in the two years of 1970 and 1971 which were so decisive for the international monetary system.

How Flexible Were Exchange Rates?

So far in this chapter I have assumed a given fixed-exchange-rate system. But while rates were not floating before March 1973 (except for the brief period from August to December 1971), they were certainly not immutably fixed. Countries were free to appreciate, and to some extent they did. Perhaps they did it belatedly, inadequately, and sometimes under pressure. But one cannot really describe that system as a fixed-exchange-rate system. Rather, one must argue that when the United States inflated, other countries had three choices, and could have chosen various combinations of them: accumulate dollars, inflate domestically, *and appreciate*.

Given this possibility of exchange-rate appreciation, one could follow two approaches. The first approach is to suppose that countries were really quite free to alter exchange rates. One could argue that in fact the system even before August 1971 was really a flexible-rate system and not a fixed-rate one. In that case, if foreign countries chose to accumulate dollars, then presumably they must have wanted dollars. They could always have stopped the accumulation of dollars by sufficient appreciation. If their domestic inflation rates were allowed to go up, then presumably this reflected a rise in their 'desired inflation rates'. Any import of inflation must then have been purely voluntary, and none of it was inevitable.

The second approach—which is less extreme and more appealing to me and which I have already outlined in the previous chapter— is to argue that countries were inhibited about exchange-rate adjustment. Therefore they did not feel fully free to alter their exchange rates or to appreciate sufficiently. At the same time, exchange rates were certainly not immutably fixed.

In the short run, when the dollar flood first hit the world, it was more like a fixed-rate world. This then gave rise to some automatic transmission of U.S. inflation, which in turn raised inflationary expectations in foreign countries, and also—in time—generated policy responses to reduce the surpluses. But, in addition, it gave rise to reluctant exchange-rate adjustments. No doubt, if countries such as Germany and Japan had been keener to eliminate their surpluses they would have appreciated earlier and more; and to that extent the dollars they accumulated might be regarded as having been 'wanted'. But there were also additional factors that inhibited exchange-rate adjustments: historical prejudices and lack of understanding, the domestic-income-distribution implications, and so on. It was particularly important that the situation developed rather rapidly. It naturally took time for an understanding to develop of the role of exchange-rate variations as an inflation-insulating device.

Thus, neither the extreme flexible-rate model nor the extreme fixed-rate model can fully explain the actual responses of the inflation-shy countries. Countries did not attain their 'desired' inflation rates, as they would have in a flexible-rate world; but neither can the whole of the inflation they did get be regarded as the inevitable result of a fixed-rate system, since they *could* have insulated themselves much more by appreciation.

The Reserve-Currency Role and Seignorage

So far I have said nothing about the United States' role as the reserve currency country. I have simply argued that she chose to run a budget deficit which yielded a balance-of-payments deficit . . . and this then in turn caused inflation to be exported, as well as creating inflation at home. The United States differed from other countries only in this way: when most countries run a payments deficit this is financed at first by a run-down in their foreign-exchange reserves and only after a while will it lead to special loans being raised, and hence the incurring of liquid or illiquid liabilities. By contrast, in the case of the United States, the deficit was financed right from the beginning by incurring liquid liabilities.

The essential feature of the reserve-currency role is that other countries willingly hold dollars. These, it must be stressed, are not dollar notes, but are predominantly interest-earning. (Bergsten has shown that in 1972 only about 10 per cent of U.S. short-term liabilities to foreigners were non-interest-bearing.) There is no quantitative constraint on the liabilities the United States can incur, in the same way as there is a quantitative constraint on countries that depend on their foreign-exchange reserves but cannot borrow to finance deficits.

Yet the line between the reserve currency country and other countries is not really sharp, and arguably there is no line at all. The liquid liabilities that the United States incurs are not costless. The reserve-currency role does not mean that the United States has a 'licence to print international money'; she has a licence only to borrow short-term from many willing lenders at a positive market-determined rate of interest, with no quantitative limit. Similarly, when there is a world capital market, other countries can borrow to finance deficits, though perhaps at a higher rate of interest, and one that rises more rapidly as the liabilities increase. At least since 1973, the difference in this respect between the United States and other credit-worthy countries has practically disappeared.

It has been argued that the United States is able to borrow exceptionally cheaply because of her reserve-currency role. In this view it is conceded that interest is paid on dollar balances held by foreigners, but it is stressed that the interest rate is very low. The U.S. makes a monopolist's profits as the producer of the world's liquid assets. This is the 'seignorage' argument. I have my doubts about it, as have many others, for example McKinnon and Bergsten. The U.S. banking system is not a monopoly. Only the Federal Reserve has a monopoly of the production of the U.S. monetary base, but this is only a very small proportion of the total dollars held by the world. The private banking sector is highly competitive. There are no controls on interest rates in the Euro-dollar market. For these reasons one should regard the once-popular 'seignorage' argument with some scepticism, and perhaps

I should not pursue it further here. Nevertheless, perhaps it has some small validity. Perhaps the U.S. banks and the monetary and fiscal authorities have reaped some rents from the willingness of the non-U.S. world to hold dollars at fairly modest rates of interest, and the U.S. lacked a constraint on balance-of-payments deficits that governed other countries. If only to understand the implications drawn from a once popular argument, let me then concede the idea and fit it into the model presented earlier. How does the presumed ability of the U.S. to borrow cheaply from the rest of the world—to get extra real resources at little cost—affect her willingness to inflate under different exchange-rate regimes?

If the United States can take policy steps to induce the rest of the world to hold more dollars, there will then be a presumed gain to her, namely the seignorage gain. In the fixed-rate system the U.S. can indeed induce the rest of the world to hold more dollars. This follows from the model of Chapter 4. If the U.S. inflates and generates a deficit in the first instance, the reactions of other countries will be to counteract this with some of their own inflation, but not so much as to eliminate their surpluses in the short run. It therefore pays the U.S. to inflate, and hence to cause more dollars to be held by the rest of the world. The U.S. has to pay interest on these dollars, but the interest payments are less than the value of the extra resources she has obtained. It follows that, because of her reserve-currency position, it pays the U.S. to aim for a higher inflation rate than she would have otherwise.

All this only applies in the fixed-rate system. In the flexible-rate system the U.S. cannot force surpluses on other countries. They will have whatever surpluses they want, achieving this by appropriate exchange-rate adjustments combined with their desired inflation rates. Thus U.S. inflation is not a way of increasing seignorage gains in the flexible-rate system. In the fixed-rate system there is then an asymmetry created by the U.S. reserve-currency role. While deficits incurred by other countries yield them losses at the margin—the net costs of accommodating capital movements—deficits incurred by the U.S. yield her net gains, at least up to some point. Thus other potential deficit countries will reduce their inflation rates below their desired ones in order to avoid or reduce deficits, while by contrast the U.S. will raise her inflation rate above her desired one in order to generate deficits.

This conclusion must now be integrated into the main model.

Let us suppose that in the flexible-rate system the U.S. would choose a 3-per-cent inflation rate and the rest of the world (which I treat here as one country) would choose 6 per cent. These are the 'desired' inflation rates. The argument in Chapter 4 was that in the fixed-rate system the U.S. would choose a higher rate, say 4 per cent, and the rest of world a lower rate, say 5 per cent, and the tendency would be for the two rates to come together. Now we get the result that the U.S. would have a reason to run an inflation rate higher than that of other countries—so as to get a deficit—in the fixed-rate system. We might then end up with the rest of the world running an inflation rate somewhat above its desired rate—say 7 per cent—and the U.S. running an inflation rate of 8 per cent. If the U.S. had been the inflation-prone country initially, while the rest of the world was relatively inflation-shy, the introduction of the seignorage effect would raise the inflation rates of both, but in the case of the rest of the world would not necessarily make its inflation rate higher than it would be in the flexible-rate system. Thus in general one can only say that world inflation will be some-what higher in the fixed-rate system because of the gains the reserve-currency country derives from seignorage.

Does the Reserve-Currency Role Depend on the Exchange-Rate Regime?

Here I should note a matter that has confused me and others in the past. I have *not* said that the reserve-currency role of the U.S. is the result of having a fixed-rate system, and would disappear with a flexible-rate system. The argument applies if we assume that the U.S. is the reserve-currency country under both types of regime. Under both regimes the U.S. has an incentive to get other countries to hold more dollars (given the seignorage argument). But the point is that only under the fixed-rate regime will U.S. inflation achieve the desired result.

The question of whether the reserve-currency role depends at all on the nature of the exchange-rate regime is really not central to this chapter. But let me say a few words on it. In the fixed-rate system a high proportion of the dollars will be held officially, and will be used to cover balance-of-payments deficits until adjust-ments through inflationary and deflationary policies have been made. In the floating-rate system there may be less official demand for dollars. But there will still be some official intervention to smooth out fluctuations, to moderate effects of shocks on real consumption levels, and so on. There is still need for official foreign-exchange reserves. In the system of managed flexibility which we have actually had since March 1973 there has, indeed, been a considerable reduction in the real value of official dollar balances held by the non-OPEC countries as a whole, and some reduction for the world as a whole. But there is clearly still a big demand for official balances—satisfied by a large increase in nominal balances in 1974.

A more important point, argued convincingly by McKinnon, is that in a floating-rate system there will be more private demand for dollars, so that the net result of a shift from a fixed to a flexible-rate system is to lower the ratio of official to private dollar holdings, without necessarily lowering the total. But I shall not expound his argument here, as the issues are peripheral to my main discussion.

The Inflation Tax: A Doubtful Argument

Finally, I want to discuss a quite distinct argument which also says that the United States has an incentive to inflate more than otherwise because of her reserve-currency role. This argument originated with Robert Mundell.

The argument runs essentially as follows. Other countries hold dollars as money. The real value of this money depends on the world price-level in the fixed-rate system (and hence is greatly influenced by the U.S. price-level), while it depends directly on the U.S. price-level in the flexible-rate system. It is then in the interests of the U.S. to raise her price-level so as to reduce the real value of these liabilities of hers. This is the argument for an inflation tax. But the greater the inflation, the less the world will want to hold dollars. The U.S. is making a seignorage profit on being the world's supplier of money. While this profit per dollar will rise when the inflation tax reduces the real value of a dollar, the number of dollars held will fall. There will then be an optimal rate of tax—in fact, a maximum revenue tax—at which U.S. seignorage is maximized. The main point is that some U.S. inflation will yield a seignorage gain through the reduction in the real value of a previously acquired stock of dollars.

The argument seems to be fallacious, at least in the simple way in which it has been put. The fallacy is the implicit assumption that foreigners hold dollar notes. Actually, as pointed out earlier, they hold interest-bearing deposits or bills (with a very small proportion non-interest-bearing). If the nominal interest rate varies with inflation, so that the real rate is a true equilibrium one, there will be no seignorage gain from taxing real balances. Greater U.S. and world inflation will simply lead to higher nominal rates, as indeed has happened. On the other hand, this type of inflation tax could arise in the short-term if the nominal rate lags behind the inflation rate, so that the real rate of interest falls with inflation, perhaps because inflationary expectations are lower than the inflation that finally turns out or because of institutional rigidities and elements of money illusion in the short run. This is the basis of the inflation tax within a country, and could lead to an international inflation tax on Mundellian lines. But it is a disequilibrium phenomenon, and is not well represented by a model which assumes a rigidly zero nominal rate of interest.

While the Mundell argument is also connected with seignorage, it should be clearly distinguished from the earlier argument that I expounded at length. The earlier argument was that the real rate of interest which the U.S. has to pay on dollar deposits, Treasury Bills, and so on, may be less than the marginal value of the extra resources to her. She might then choose in a fixed-exchange-rate system to inflate somewhat more than otherwise in order to generate a balance-of-payments deficit so as to obtain these extra resources. In this case the real rate of interest is assumed to be low but not necessarily to fall with inflation. By contrast, in the Mundell argument the real rate of interest falls because of inflation owing to a rigidity in the nominal rate.

REFERENCES

The 'monetarist' exposition of the causes of world inflation (as originating in the U.S.) can be found in many papers by Harry Johnson, R. A. Mundell, and others. One reference is Harry G. Johnson, 'World Inflation and the International Monetary System', *The Three Banks Review* (September 1975), 3–22. An article that influenced this chapter at a late stage is H. Robert Heller, 'International Reserves and World-wide Inflation', *Staff Papers*, 23 (March 1976), 61–87. A survey article on the role of the dollar, with many references, is Marina v. N. Whitman, 'The Current and Future Role of the Dollar: How Much Symmetry', *Brookings Papers on Economic Activity*, 3 (1974), 539–91; see also the discussion following this paper. Finally, for a valuable survey of facts and issues, and the monetarist interpretation, see Harold van B. Cleveland and Bruce Brittain, *The Great Inflation: A Monetarist View*, National Planning Association, Washington, 1976.

Excellent accounts of international monetary developments relevant to the discussion here can be found in the various *Annual Reports* of the Bank for International Settlements. Most figures in this chapter come from *International Financial Statistics* (published by the International Monetary Fund) or from Heller's article.

An important article on the seignorage concept is Herbert G. Grubel, 'The Distribution of Seignorage from International Liquidity Creation' in R. A. Mundell and A. Swoboda (eds.), *Monetary Problems of the International Economy*, University of Chicago Press, 1969 (see also in the same book the paper by Harry G. Johnson on this subject, and the general discussion). An important and convincing paper, critical of the seignorage approach is Ronald I. McKinnon, *Private and International Money: The Case for the Dollar*, Essays in International Finance No. 74, Princeton, 1969. See also a survey of the seignorage issues and relevant data in C. Fred Bergsten, *The Dilemmas of the Dollar*, Council on Foreign Relations (New York, 1975) 209–215. The argument by Mundell about the inflation tax is in R. A. Mundell, 'The Optimum Balance of Payments Deficit', in E. Claassen and P. Salin (eds.), *Stabilization Policies in Interdependent Economies*, North-Holland, Amsterdam, 1972.

INTERNATIONAL ADJUSTMENT
TO THE OIL-PRICE RISE

7

THE ADJUSTMENT TO THE OIL-PRICE
RISE: INCOME DISTRIBUTION,
INFLATION, AND UNEMPLOYMENT

I N this chapter I want to look analytically at the main effects of
the rise in the oil price, especially from a short-run macro-economic
point of view. I shall attempt to provide a framework of analysis—
to classify the various effects. The world will be treated as if it
consisted of only two countries—the oil exporters (OPEC) and the
Rest; the world of many countries will be introduced in the next
chapter. Furthermore, I shall not focus on balance of payments
and exchange-rate implications at this stage, this also being left
for the next chapter.

The oil-price rise came on top of a world inflation that was well
on the way beforehand and that clearly had its own momentum.
So one cannot assume that all or even most of the disturbances of
1974 and 1975 can be blamed on oil. There has been a tendency to
overrate the importance of the oil-price rise. It follows that it is
not sufficient to look at the facts of 1974 and 1975, and compare
them with earlier years, to see what the oil-price rise actually did.
One really must theorize first, to see what might have happened
and might have been expected if other things had stayed equal.
And this is what I shall do in this chapter and the next. But in
Chapter 9 I shall take a brief look at what actually happened, and
ask to what extent various actual developments can be attributed
to oil. I shall also look at the effects of the oil-price rise on international liquidity and on the question of whether there was any
need for countries to agree on any 'current account targets', or
indeed on any macro-economic policies.

A World of Smooth Adjustment: Income Distribution Effects

Let me begin then by treating the world as if it consisted of only
two countries, OPEC and the Rest. The Rest actually consists of

O.E.C.D. and the less-developed countries but this distinction is not going to be particularly important. I assume that there is complete flexibility of prices and wages. This is, of course, only a start. Now OPEC raises the price of oil that its members sell. This is as if OPEC had imposed an excise tax on consumers of its oil. I shall assume also that all income is spent immediately by OPEC and that also in the Rest any changes in income lead immediately to equivalent spending changes. Discussion of macro-economic problems will thus be postponed.

The oil-price rise will have three types of income-distribution effects. The *primary* income-distribution effect is the redistribution from the Rest to OPEC. This is certainly the main effect, representing a significant world redistribution of income. Essentially it is the equivalent of the revenue effect of an excise tax. But, as will be shown below, the gain received by OPEC will be somewhat less than the loss incurred by the Rest if consumption of OPEC oil is reduced as a result of the price rise. The *secondary* income distribution effect is a redistribution within the Rest and results from the prices of substitutes for OPEC oil rising and the prices of complements falling. Obvious substitutes are the oil produced within the Rest as well as other sources of energy, such as coal and natural gas. Transport services and motor cars are complements. Finally, there is the *tertiary* income-distribution effect. It is also a redistribution within the Rest and results from the changed spending pattern brought about by the primary and secondary income-distribution effects. Thus producers of goods especially favoured by OPEC buyers may gain incomes while producers of income-elastic goods consumed by the Rest's energy consumers or by producers of oil-complementary goods, will lose.

These income distribution effects are central to the analysis of the oil-price rise in the short run. Even in a world of smooth adjustment they create problems, in fact the problems of adjusting to lower incomes by the various losers. This is particularly so when the incomes are already desperately low, as in the case of some less-developed countries.

Apart from the redistribution of world income there will also be some over-all effect: it can be shown that world income as a whole is likely to fall—so that gainers could not compensate losers even if they wanted to and still have something left over. A lot could be said about this over-all effect. But for the present purposes I need only be brief: I am mainly concerned with the short-run effects and the over-all effects are not so significant in the short run.

This over-all effect has a consumption substitution and a production substitution component.[1] Consider first the consumption-substitution cost. Consumers of energy will economize on energy. There will be three possible elements of loss from the decline in the consumption of energy. Firstly, OPEC producers will lose rent on the oil output foregone; this assumes that the cost of production and opportunity cost of this oil (in terms of its value in later years) was less than its price initially. Secondly, there is a loss of tax revenue to the Rest's governments. Thirdly, consumers will use income at the margin for less preferred alternatives to energy use. In addition, there is the production substitution cost. More expensive energy substitutes will replace OPEC oil, at least at the margin. In time—as North Sea oil production gets under way, as the world coal industry revives, and so on—this could be a very significant and very wasteful effect from the point of view of the world as a whole. The necessary investment is indeed now under way, so that some of the resource cost is being incurred now.

Introducing Savings and Investment

In the short run gainers will tend to save more and losers save less or even dissave. These effects were at the centre of discussion in 1974. The increase in savings by OPEC countries was vast, as is well known. The gainers included not only the OPEC countries but also the producers of domestic oil in countries such as the United States, and in these cases also, savings may have increased in the short run. On the other hand, many firms all round the world reduced their savings, and even dissaved. In addition, governments in countries hard hit by the oil-price rise ran budget deficits, and so dissaved. In general this reflected a deliberate attempt to sustain, or at least avoid drastic falls in, national consumption levels. In fact, the main increase in savings attributable to the oil-price rise was by OPEC governments and the main dissaving has probably been by the Rest's governments. But increased savings by U.S. private oil producers, and decreased savings by various private firms, for example in the motor-car industry, may also have been important.

[1] See Appendix I (p. 109 below) for a geometric exposition of the argument in this paragraph.

At the same time there were changes in investment demand. Emphasis was usually put on the extra investment demand coming from the energy industries, and it was sometimes argued that this was more than enough to absorb the extra savings generated by OPEC. But one must bear in mind that while industries competitive with OPEC oil became prospectively more profitable and hence generated new investment demand, industries complementary with energy—notably the motor-car industry, but also tourism—will have generated less investment demand as a result.

For the moment I am still assuming smooth adjustment, and postponing discussion of monetary problems, wage rigidities, and so on. The position then is that a new equilibrium will be established in the capital market, probably but not inevitably with more savings and investment. If one takes the view that was common originally, that the whole story is dominated by the vast rise in OPEC savings, the result is a rise in world savings which brings down the real rate of interest and so leads to higher world investment.

These savings and investment effects are the consequences of the income distribution effects of the oil-price rise: gainers save more, losers dissave or save less; gaining industries attract investment funds and losing industries become less attractive. But the net result may be to generate further income distribution effects. First, when OPEC governments invest in private securities in the Rest the return they get is much less than the marginal social rate of return on the relevant investment because of taxation of profits. Thus the Rest's governments will retrieve part of the original national losses resulting from the oil-price rise. The gains will go mainly to those governments in the Rest whose countries have the more extensive private investment opportunities, and with corporate taxes usually 40–50 per cent the gains should be significant.

The second income-distribution effect arises if the real rate of interest has to change in order to restore capital market equilibrium. If one again supposes that the increase in OPEC savings dominates the story, then the real rate of interest will fall, and there could be a major redistribution of income and capital values within the Rest as a result. New debtors gain and creditors lose. Thus the British Government was a big borrower in 1974, its deficit not being explained solely by the oil-price rise, and it undoubtedly benefited from the availability of ample and cheap credit on the world capital market. At the same time there will be various effects on capital values which I shall not go into here. Essentially owners of capital assets will gain and 'old' borrowers will lose.

The Capital Market

These developments have various implications for the capital market which gave rise to lots of worries in 1974. But in fact the market was shown to work well, as indeed might have been expected.

First, the total business of the market suddenly expanded, not just because total world savings increased but even more because some governments (of OPEC) increased their savings while others (in the Rest) borrowed to finance dissaving. There was a danger that the major banks were under-capitalized for this increase in the flow of funds.

Secondly, governments became large borrowers and lenders on the market, something that had not been too common in recent years. Private banks found themselves having to assess the credit-worthiness of many governments. This flow of official funds through the market also raised questions about the meaning of balance-of-payments deficits and international liquidity. Could one regard borrowing by the U.K. government, or lending by the Saudi government, as autonomous or accommodating, for example? I shall come back to this issue in Chapter 9.

Thirdly, one had the unusual situation where there was large-scale borrowing by governments for consumption maintenance, rather than investment, which raised a particular question in the minds of bankers about credit-worthiness.

Finally, there was a special problem about the term structure of lending and borrowing. The OPEC countries wanted to lend short —very short—while borrowers generally wanted to borrow medium or long term, so there was a banking job, involving considerable risks, to be done. Naturally the market dealt with this by providing appropriate interest rate differentials, and the OPEC governments concerned gradually adapted their lending to the situation.

I don't think I need to go into all this further. It is clear that this particular market worked as well as any Chicago economist might have wished and would have expected. But it is worth noting that in 1974 many bankers had far less confidence in its ability to do so than did market-oriented economists.

Introducing Money: Cost-Inflationary and Demand-Deflationary Effects[1]

Let us now assume that money wages are rigid downwards. At the same time we assume, provisionally, that real wages are flexible. We thus move into a traditional Keynesian-type model. The central question is whether the oil-price rise is inflationary or deflationary. For the moment let me assume away an active fiscal policy. We suppose either that tax rates and government expenditure are kept constant, or that the budget deficit is kept constant, possibly at zero. The only policy instrument is then variation of the money supply. As earlier, I tell the story in stages.

In stage I, I assume that monetary policy keeps the real rate of interest constant. The oil-price rise shifts world income distribution towards high savers, namely the OPEC countries. I shall assume that dissaving by the private sector is not sufficient to offset this. Furthermore, while there may be some extra investment demand from the Rest's energy sector, this also is not sufficient to offset the rise in savings. Hence aggregate demand falls, the initial fall being aggravated by a multiplier. Thus the oil-price rise is deflationary at this stage. This is the aspect of the oil-price rise which was much emphasized in 1974 and 1975 and is clearly important. In effect, the OPEC countries taxed the Rest's oil consumers, and a substantial part of the tax revenue was not spent by them. It must be repeated here that we are assuming a particular type of monetary policy, namely one that keeps the real rate of interest constant. Furthermore, there is not an active fiscal policy.

At the same time, the general price-level will have risen. The prices of oil and of oil substitutes, and of products into which oil is an input directly or indirectly, have risen, but because of money-wage rigidity downwards, the prices of other goods cannot have fallen. With money-wage rigidity downwards, any relative-price change must raise the average price-level. Because of this effect, the oil-price rise is generally described as being *cost*-inflationary— even though it is also *demand*-deflationary. But the price-rise effect is a once-for-all one, so it may not be right to describe it as

[1] See Appendix II (p. 111 below) for a geometric exposition of the argument of this section.

'inflationary'. We shall see later that it may indeed give rise to a continuous or prolonged price rise, in which case the term inflation would be more appropriate.

Now I come to stage II of the argument. The real rate of interest is no longer assumed to be kept constant; rather the *nominal* money supply is constant. In that case the net effects on aggregate demand and on the rate of interest depend on three factors.

First, as just pointed out, the increased world propensity to save (not fully offset by increased investment demand) reduces aggregate demand and hence income; this in turn will now reduce the demand for money, which in turn reduces the rate of interest, which stimulates investment, and so modifies the initial fall in demand. Thus demand falls, but not as much as in the stage I case, and the real rate of interest falls. Secondly, the higher price-level reduces the real value of the given nominal money supply. This reduced real money supply also has a deflationary effect, but *raises* the rate of interest. Thirdly, it is possible that income distribution has shifted towards governments with a relatively higher demand for money, or at least liquidity, so that more money stays idle; this has the same effect as a reduction in the real money supply. We find then that at this stage, with the nominal money supply constant, the oil-price rise is certainly demand-deflationary (and, if we like, cost-inflationary) but the real rate of interest could have risen or fallen.

In stage III we can suppose that monetary policy is so manipulated as to restore the level of aggregate demand. This will require a rise in the nominal money supply for three reasons: to offset the effects of the higher savings propensity; to offset the effects of the price rise; and to offset the effects of the (possible) shift towards those holders of money that have an exceptionally high liquidity preference. Finally the real rate of interest will be lower than it was initially, as one would expect when there was, at a constant rate of interest and constant income, an increase in savings greater than the increase in investment demand. And also, finally, the real-money supply will be higher than it was initially.

The conclusion then is that both at a constant rate of interest and with a constant nominal money supply the effect of the oil-price rise will be demand-deflationary. In fact, the two assumptions could lead to exactly the same result, though they need not. The restoration of 'internal balance' requires both the nominal and the real-money supply to increase, and the real rate of interest to fall. All this ignores the possible use of fiscal policy.

Fiscal Policy

The fiscal deficits induced in some countries by the oil-price rise can be thought of as having two motivations or components.

The first component represents the response to the cost-inflationary effect of the oil-price rise. Governments choose to dis-save or to reduce their savings in order to moderate the adverse real-income effects of the oil-price rise at the first stage, before full macro-economic repercussions are taken into account. Thus governments might be thought of as being like firms or households. They react to a sudden fall in real incomes brought about by a rise in the cost of oil and oil substitutes by moderating the adverse effects on public and private consumption. A budget deficit makes it possible to maintain the real value of government expenditures* and perhaps to subsidize private consumption through devices such as food subsidies. This particular fiscal response can then be included in the net effect on savings we discussed earlier. This response was undoubtedly important in 1974 in some countries, such as Britain, though not in others (U.S., Japan, France).

The second component of the fiscal deficits is the response to the demand-deflationary effect of the oil-price rise. It is designed to work together with monetary policy to restore 'internal balance'. The more fiscal policy rather than monetary policy is used for this purpose, the less the real rate of interest needs to fall finally, and it is even possible that it rises. If the nominal money supply were held completely constant, the real rate of interest would finally have to rise. In actual fact, in most countries the nominal money supply increased, but not sufficiently to keep the real money supply constant, there was some fiscal expansion, especially in 1975, and the real rate of interest fell. But these net results were not, as we shall see in Chapter 9, by any means wholly attributable to the oil-price rise.

Wage Rigidity and Secondary Cost Inflation

So far we have assumed that real wages are flexible, though money wages are rigid downwards. Suppose, as an extreme case, that *real* wages rather than money wages were utterly inflexible

downwards. Monetary policy could not then maintain full employment. The oil-price rise brings about a redistribution of income
which in a flexible world requires some real wages to fall. If,
instead, they refuse to fall, there will be some inevitable unemployment of the relevant factors irrespective of monetary policy.
Looking at the Rest as a whole, the oil-price rise brings about a fall
in its full employment real income, a fall which would be borne by
various sectors of the community, different kinds of wage-earners,
capitalists, beneficiaries of government expenditure, and so on. If
some sections refuse to accept the required fall in real-wage rates
or in disposable income per head, there will then be unemployment
—unless there are deliberate redistributive measures which load
the whole adverse impact onto other, more flexible, sections.

This is the extreme case where some real wages are completely
rigid downwards. The Phillips curve is vertical. The oil-price rise
has shifted the curve to the right, raising the 'natural' rate of
unemployment. But perhaps a more realistic approach would be to
assume that there is *some* 'real wage resistance', but not necessarily
sufficient to keep the real wage rigid, and subject to some pressure
from the rate of unemployment.

The oil-price rise then has the initial effect on costs and prices
that we have already described. This is the *primary* cost-inflation
effect. This, in turn, gives rise to increases in money wages
designed to restore, at least partially, the level of real wages. So
there is also a *secondary* cost inflation. The latter is not just once
and for all, since the higher wages further raise the price-level,
hence give rise to further increases in money wages, and so on. This
secondary effect may or may not come to an end before the real-
wage level has been restored.

If the nominal money supply is not increased the effect of this
secondary cost inflation, as of the primary one, will be demand-
deflationary. Governments can certainly increase the nominal money
supply if they think this is desirable. So the relevant implication is
that they may *choose* not to restore the level of real demand to its
original level, and may deliberately generate some extra unemployment in order to inhibit the secondary cost-inflation effect. One may
conclude that unemployment may result either because the real
wage is rigid downwards or because some fall in this real wage can
only be brought about by an increase in unemployment that is at
least temporary. With money wages responding to higher prices,

any fall in the real wage can only be brought about by a prolonged price–wage–price spiral.

At the same time it must be remembered that the oil-price rise which initiated the whole process must be seen as a *real* price rise. There would be no problem for the Rest if the real impact of the rise in the dollar price of oil could be fully inflated away by raising the money prices of the goods the Rest sells to OPEC. While there was some short-term effect of this kind, mitigating the original impact, the sensible assumption is that in due course the dollar price of oil will be adjusted to attain the real level desired by OPEC.

APPENDIX I

THE WELFARE EFFECTS OF THE
OIL-PRICE RISE

In Figure 3 the horizontal axis shows the quantity of energy produced and consumed in the Rest and the vertical axis shows price, marginal cost, etc. The diagram is a somewhat over-simplified representation of some of the issues.

The curve D_1 is the demand curve for energy by users and shows the marginal private and social valuation of various quantities. The curve D_2 allows for taxes on energy use, above all the gasoline tax. The vertical distance between D_1 and D_2 is the tax, and D_2 is the tax-adjusted demand curve by users. (It is assumed here that the tax is the same on energy irrespective of whether it is produced in the Rest or imported from OPEC.)

The curve s is the energy supply curve in the Rest; from the point of view of the Rest as a whole, it represents import-competing production. OT is the initial price of energy (oil) imports from OPEC, and OT' is the higher price after the great price rise. OR is the cost to OPEC of its

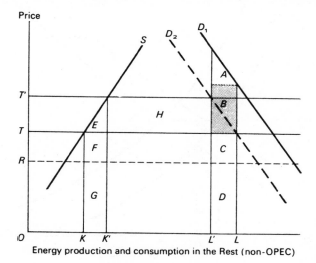

Energy production and consumption in the Rest (non-OPEC)

FIG 3

exports, this cost including the present value of sales revenue foregone in future years by taking the oil out of the ground now.

Before the price rise, the Rest consumes OL of energy, produces OK within the Rest and so imports KL from OPEC. The price rise causes consumption to fall by L'L and the Rest's production to increase by KK', so that imports from OPEC fall to K'L'.

The welfare loss of the consumption fall is the consumer valuation of this oil (indicated by willingness to pay; i.e. area under the demand curve D_1), namely $(A+B+C+D)$ less the cost of it to OPEC, D. This loss has three components: the cost to consumers of using income for less preferred purposes, A (the consumer surplus loss), the tax loss to the Rest's governments, B (shaded in the diagram), and the rent loss to OPEC, C.

The welfare loss of the production increase in the Rest is the opportunity cost of the extra energy produced there (indicated by the area under the supply curve, assumed to show marginal cost at various outputs), namely $(E+F+G)$ less the cost of the output foregone by OPEC, G. This loss has two components, the excess cost of production over the original price E, a loss borne by the Rest, and the rent loss to OPEC, F.

In addition, there is the pure redistributive effect H, equivalent to the revenue from an excise tax. There will be a net gain to OPEC provided H is greater than $(C+F)$.

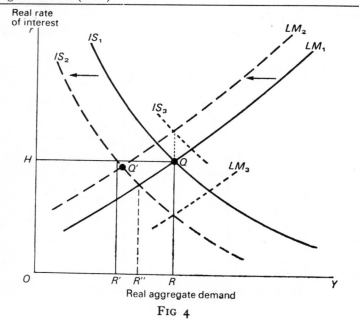

FIG 4

THE EFFECTS OF THE OIL-PRICE RISE IN THE *LM-IS* DIAGRAM

Figure 4 (see opposite) represents the standard Hicks–Hansen LM–IS diagram. It is applied here to the world as a whole. The horizontal axis shows *real* aggregate demand and the vertical axis the real rate of interest. Each LM curve assumes the real money supply to be constant and the world demand for money function to be unchanged. Initially, the relevant LM curve is LM_1 and the relevant IS curve is IS_1; equilibrium is at Q, the level of demand being OR and the rate of interest OH.

The increase in the world propensity to save owing to the redistribution of world income towards high savers shifts the IS curve to IS_2. Any increase in investment demand would shift the curve in the opposite direction, but we assume the net effect is to shift the IS curve to the left, as shown by the arrow. If monetary policy kept the real rate of interest constant (the LM curve moving the appropriate distance to the left), demand would fall to OR'.

If monetary policy had kept the LM curve unchanged, and so allowed the rate of interest to fall, and hence to stimulate extra investment, demand would only have fallen to R''.

If the nominal money supply is constant the price rise lowers the real money supply. In addition the demand for money may have risen because holdings have shifted to governments with high liquidity preference; these two effects shift the LM curve to the left, as shown by the arrow, namely to LM_2. The new equilibrium is at Q'. Demand has fallen both because of the IS shift and the LM shift; the rate of interest may have risen or fallen (in the diagram the IS shift is larger, so the rate of interest has fallen).

If monetary policy on its own were used to restore the original level of real demand, the LM curve would shift to LM_3, so that the real money supply would finally be higher than it was initially, while the rate of interest would be lower. If the job had been done by fiscal policy on its own (with the nominal money supply staying constant), the IS curve would have been shifted to IS_3. Of course, various combinations of monetary and fiscal policy are possible. Furthermore, these policies might not restore demand to the original level, perhaps deliberately so as to inhibit a cost-inflationary process.

REFERENCES

Many important and relevant papers are in Edward R. Fried and Charles L. Schultze (eds.), *Higher Oil Prices and the World Economy*, Brookings Institution, Washington, 1975, which is the best single book on the general subject of this and the next two chapters (see especially the paper by John Williamson). Full accounts of how the world capital market coped with the effects of the oil-price rise are in the 1975 and 1976 *Annual Reports* of the Bank for International Settlements. This chapter and the next are based to some extent on W. M. Corden, 'The Effects of the Oil Price Rise on the International Economy', in M. Artis and R. Nobay (eds.), *Essays in Economic Analysis*, Cambridge University Press, 1976, a paper that deals with some issues more fully and rigorously.

8

THE ADJUSTMENT TO THE OIL-PRICE RISE: BALANCES OF PAYMENTS AND EXCHANGE-RATE FLEXIBILITY

In this chapter I shall look at balance-of-payments implications of the oil-price rise and the role of exchange rates.

One can begin with a very simple point. For the Rest as a whole there is really no balance-of-payments problem as a result of the oil-price rise. The value of imports from OPEC goes up; then OPEC countries use part of their extra income to buy the Rest's exports; the net result is a current account deficit for the Rest. But the remainder of OPEC's extra income must go somewhere. It will be—indeed, has been—deposited in the Rest's banks, lent to the Rest's governments, and so on. It must come back to the Rest as autonomous capital movements. Thus the Rest as a whole finds that its capital-account surplus equals its current-account deficit. If OPEC had taken a significant part of payments in the form of gold and previously existing SDRs, a net overall deficit for the Rest would have emerged. But OPEC has not. Statistically, a deficit for the Rest is recorded when some of the short-term deposits of OPEC in the Rest's banks are described as accommodating rather than autonomous. (I return to this statistical issue in Chapter 9.) But in practice OPEC countries had no choice but to put their surpluses somewhere in the Rest (aside from acquiring gold), so that the Rest as a whole did not explicitly have to engage in accommodating borrowing.

The balance-of-payments problem therefore arises only when one looks at the differential impact on different countries within the Rest.

Balance-of-Payments Effects: Current Accounts

Let us assume for a moment that money wages in the different countries in the Rest are constant. Of course this assumption will have to be removed shortly. Further, exchange rates are fixed. In addition, in each country 'internal balance' is maintained by appropriate monetary and fiscal policies. The oil-price rise now has a variety of effects on the current accounts of the countries in the Rest. For any particular country one might distinguish the primary from the secondary effects.

The current account will worsen because of the extra cost of oil imports from OPEC. On the other hand it will improve because of extra exports (visible and invisible) to OPEC. The net result one might describe as the primary deficit (sometimes described as the 'oil deficit'), and the sum of all the primary deficits will add up to the total OPEC surplus. In addition there are the secondary deficits and surpluses. A country that imports substitutes for oil—coal or natural gas—may have a secondary deficit, and a country that exports these may have a surplus. The reverse applies to complements. Countries that export goods that are income elastic in the Rest may get deficits, and so on. Secondary deficits and surpluses add up algebraically to zero for the Rest.

Taking primary and secondary effects together, it is thus possible for an individual country in the Rest actually to go into surplus, but in general one would expect the primary deficits to dominate. Countries that are big importers of OPEC oil and that are not able to offset the cost of this with large increases in exports to OPEC will have the large deficits.

Balance-of-Payments Effects: Capital Accounts

To get the full balance-of-payments effects at constant exchange rates one must then add in the capital-account surpluses. OPEC members deposit funds in dollars, sterling, Swiss francs, and so on. They lend to some developing countries, and to others, such as Japan. They invest in various ways. But it is not sufficient to look only at where these funds go in the first instance. Capital markets, especially the New York and the Euro-dollar markets, are not the final resting homes for these funds. For example, private firms and governments outside the United States borrow on the New York market. The capital will flow finally to those countries where private firms appear to have investment opportunities for the funds, and where governments have chosen to borrow, perhaps for consumption maintenance.

It is really impossible at this point to distinguish autonomous from accommodating borrowing by governments. A government may borrow to sustain consumption and the level of expenditure, including investment expenditure in the public sector. In spite of this, its country may be left with an over-all deficit. So its foreign exchange reserves run down. Perhaps the government then borrows more to stop a further run-down. This might be called accommodating borrowing, since it avoids the immediate necessity of devaluation. But if the government had borrowed on, say, the Euro-dollar market before the foreign-exchange reserves ran down, and perhaps in order to stop them running down, was that not accommodating?

I shall come back to the question of what one means by a balance-of-payments deficit and surplus, and by international liquidity, in the next chapter, and I already referred to it in Chapter 3. But at this point we can arrive at the interim situation where various countries have current-account deficits, and some or all have capital-account surpluses. The over-all balance of payments then goes into deficit for some countries and into surplus for others, and for the Rest as a whole these over-all deficits and surpluses add up algebraically to zero. Thus the over-all balance-of-payments problem is a problem *within* the Rest.

How then do countries adjust to these imbalances? In the short term they may do so by variation in reserves and in accommodating borrowing, but eventually they must do so either by deflation and inflation, as appropriate, or by exchange rate adjustment, combined with the appropriate increase or decrease in absorption.

Balance-of-Payments Effects, Borrowing, and the Exchange Rate: An Example

To see more precisely how all this works out, and especially to see what happens to real wages, let me spell out an example here. We have three countries in the Rest, which I shall call India, Britain, and Norway. (I am not describing precisely the actual experiences of these three countries). They are all small countries in the Rest, which is dominated by the United States. Money wages are constant in all three (this assumption will certainly have to be removed shortly). Initially each country incurs a current-account deficit because of the oil-price rise, and a deflationary gap at a constant real-interest rate. The real-interest rate is given from outside—on the world market—and does not change. The argument would not be altered if it were allowed to fall somewhat. With money wages constant and prices higher because of the oil-price rise, real wages fall in all three countries.

India receives no extra private capital inflow and its government chooses not to borrow, or is unable to borrow. In reality India did, of course, get some assistance, but it certainly was not enough. So India goes into over-all deficit. Britain receives a little private-capital inflow, but covers the remainder of the potential deficit by public borrowing, which is then used to finance public consumption, tax reductions, food subsidies, and so on. Norway receives a large inflow of private capital, sufficient to put the over-all balance into surplus. She does not find it necessary to borrow publicly at all.

Let us now look at each of the three cases. India has a deficit and a deflationary gap. So she devalues. This switches expenditure away from foreign goods on to Indian goods, hence reducing or eliminating both the deficit and the deflationary gap. While the original terms of trade deterioration lowered real wages, the devaluation is likely to do so further. Finally, real wages will certainly have fallen, real expenditure having adjusted to the lower real income resulting from the oil-price rise.

Britain (in this example!) does not need to devalue, since her government has borrowed to cover the current account deficit. If this deficit is then used to finance the maintenance of real public spending which benefits wage-earners (keeping up the 'social wage'), to cut taxes so as to compensate wage-earners to some extent for the higher oil prices, and perhaps to subsidize the cost of living through food subsidies, then the real wage—defined as the after-tax wage and to include the 'social wage'—need not fall at all. No loss is incurred currently. The burden of the oil-price rise is shifted on to taxpayers in the future.

Norway also starts off with a deficit and a deflationary gap, and a fall in real wages. But in this case private-capital inflow leading to extra investment expenditures in Norway more than compensates. Before the exchange rate alters or money wages rise it has a surplus and excess demand domestically. Hence its money wages have to rise or it has to appreciate in order to switch spending away from non-traded to traded goods and production from traded to non-traded goods. The original terms of trade deterioration will have lowered real wages; the appreciation is likely to have raised real wages. But total spending for consumption will certainly have fallen, so it is likely that on balance real wages have finally fallen.

In looking at these three examples the most interesting point to notice is that Britain did not need to alter her exchange rate and her real-wage level remained unchanged, while India depreciated and Norway appreciated, but in the case of India the real wage certainly fell and in the case of Norway it probably fell. In the case of Norway there was a rise in real absorption, made possible by the capital inflow, but this was absorption for investment, not consumption, so that real consumption fell.

Relative Prices and Exchange Rates: What Really Happened

Money wages rather obviously have *not* stayed constant. They have risen at very different rates. They have risen for a variety of reasons that have nothing at all to do with the oil-price rise; after all, the great inflation was well under way before October 1973. But they also rose to some extent *because* of the oil-price rise. This was the *secondary* cost-inflation effect referred to earlier.

This secondary cost-inflation effect varied between countries for essentially two reasons: first, the adverse real-wage effects of the oil-price rise differed, and secondly, government attitudes to cost inflation and the appropriateness of deliberate counter-inflationary policies of deflation differed. The varying dependence of different countries on imported oil certainly helps to explain differences in wage-inflation rates in 1974—notably why Japan and Italy had such high inflation rates—but varying government attitudes explain much more the later differences—why Germany's inflation rate was so low, why Japan's came down so rapidly, and why Britain's stayed up and even accelerated.

Fixed exchange rates would have been an impossibility in this situation. The actual exchange-rate variations that took place over the relevant period 1973–5 can be regarded, broadly, as having had three components. Firstly, there were fluctuations in response to short-term capital movements, essentially speculative portfolio adjustments. These certainly explain the considerable variations in the crucial dollar-D-mark rate, and some part of the general tendency to appreciate of the Swiss franc. Secondly, there were the variations in the exchange rates which compensated for the different rates of change of factor costs per unit of output—depending in this particular period mainly on differences in rates of change in money wages. This element of exchange-rate adjustment maintained constant the competitiveness of the import-competing and export industries of different countries. Thirdly, there were changes which altered competitiveness over the period as a whole, and—in the case of countries that improved their competitiveness —reflected deliberate attempts through exchange-rate intervention to reduce relevant current-account deficits.

The first component explains swings rather than trends, other than in the case of the Swiss franc. Here I want to focus on trends over the 1973–5 period. It is the distinction between the second and the third component that is then of interest.

If exchange rates had remained fixed there would have been great changes in relative competitiveness, given the different rates of change in money wages. This would have led to switching of demand patterns towards countries with low cost increases, such as Germany, and away from countries, such as Britain and Italy, with high inflation rates. Production and employment in the export and import-competing industries of the high-inflation countries would have fallen severely. These countries could, indeed, have maintained aggregate demand by fiscal, and possibly monetary, policies, but it would have involved a shift or switching of resources out of the industries producing traded goods (exportables and importables) and into the non-traded goods and services sectors. The low-wage-inflation countries, by contrast, would have had shifts and income distribution effects in the opposite direction. Of course, in time money wages might have responded to the situation—extra unemployment in the export and import-competing sectors discouraging wage-demands in the high-inflation countries—but this would have taken time, and meanwhile severe dislocation effects would have been felt, not to speak of the vast imbalances in current accounts superimposed on the primary deficits and secondary deficits and surpluses referred to earlier. So, in general, countries altered, or permitted alteration in, exchange rates to avoid these effects.

In general, *real* exchange rates—meaning competitive relationships—were not allowed to alter much. Thus, to a considerable extent, the shifts or switching that I have just described were avoided. It is fairly clear that over the period 1973–5 as a whole most changes in nominal exchange rates can be explained in these terms. (I rest here mainly on evidence given in the Annual Report of the International Monetary Fund for 1975, though this only went up to the first quarter of 1975.) The two significant exceptions appear to be Switzerland, which lost competitiveness, and Japan which probably gained. (If one had used an earlier reference point, say 1969, one would also find that the United States had gained competitiveness greatly, and by the summer of 1976 the U.K. had possibly gained competitiveness.)

The broad generalization then is that exchange rates were *not* greatly altered to avoid the need for accommodating capital movements or reserve changes. Rather, in a *real* sense they remained broadly constant over the period as a whole, even though nominal rates greatly altered, and there were of course significant short-term fluctuations. The possible reasons for this particular exchange-rate policy I shall come to in the next chapter, when discussing the question of international agreements and the need for co-ordination.

This does not mean that the current-account experience of various countries only reflected the direct impact of the oil-price rise. This would be a false conclusion. Germany ran a vast surplus in 1974 in spite of being a large importer of OPEC oil. The principal reason for the different balance-of-payments experiences was that levels of demand in relation to capacity greatly varied: in 1974 and 1975 German policy was much more deflationary than Britain's, for example. These different demand policies were also very noticeable in 1975, and explain much more of the different current account experiences, and especially the turn-arounds of Japan and Italy, than changes in competitiveness.

The Four Sources of Imbalance

At the risk of repetitiveness, I should like to draw together the various elements of current-account imbalance which I have presented so far, emphasizing the assumption on which each separate element rests.

First, we assume that (a) countries are holding their money wages and exchange rates constant, or that wages and exchange rates move together so that competitiveness does not alter—i.e. that *real* exchange rates are constant, so that there is no switching; and (b) that aggregate-demand policies maintain 'internal balance' in each country. In that case we get the *primary* deficit for each country, which expresses the immediate bilateral effect relative to OPEC countries; the sum of these primary deficits equals the OPEC current-account surplus. It might be described as the 'full-employment oil deficit'. In addition we get the *secondary* deficits and surpluses, which reflect substitution, complementary and income elasticity effects, and which cancel out for the Rest as a whole.

Next, we remove assumption (a) and allow competitiveness within the Rest to alter, so that switching results. We continue to assume internal balance policies. These changes in real exchange rates bring about *tertiary* imbalances within the Rest. My argument has been that this effect was not in general important over the period as a whole, except perhaps in the cases of Switzerland and Japan. In general, nominal exchange rates varied so as to avoid such changes in competitiveness.

Finally, we remove assumption (b), and allow some countries to run demand more below 'internal balance' levels than others; this gives these countries surpluses and the others deficits, and might be called the *quaternary* deficits or surpluses.[1] These imbalances would result even if real exchange rates stayed fixed.

As mentioned earlier, in general, countries tended to follow deflationary policies to counteract the cost-inflationary effects of the oil-price rise as well as the general cost inflation which was already under way before the oil-price rise; hence the sum of the Rest's quaternary deficits would exceed the sum of surpluses, the OPEC surplus falling as a result. The actual 'oil deficits' were thus less than the primary deficits—that is, less than the 'full-employment oil deficits'—because of the general deflation.

Looking at these four sources of imbalance it is my impression that the primary and quaternary imbalances were particularly important in 1974, and in 1975 the quaternary imbalances were in practice the most important.

---

[1] This term, not commonly used in economics, comes from geology.

REFERENCES

See, again, Edward R. Fried and Charles L. Schultze (eds.), *Higher Oil Prices and the World Economy*, Brookings Institution, Washington, 1975. On the general issues of adjustment to the oil-price rise as well as exchange-rate and reserves policies, see Thomas D. Willett, *The Oil-Transfer Problem and International Economic Stability*, Essays in International Finance No. 113, Princeton, 1975, and Weir M. Brown, *World Afloat: National Policies Ruling the Waves*, Essays in International Finance No. 116, Princeton, 1976. Also relevant for basic information and general background are the issues of the O.E.C.D. *Economic Outlook* (a bi-annual), December 1974 to July 1976.

Some estimates and discussions of what happened to *real* exchange rates are in International Monetary Fund, *Annual Report 1975*, 31–3, in the 46th *Annual Report* of the Bank for International Settlements (June 1976), 102–4, and in Federal Reserve Bank of St. Louis, *Review*, 58 (August 1976), 14.

9

ADJUSTMENT TO THE OIL-PRICE RISE: THREE INTERESTING ISSUES

IN this chapter I want to discuss three interesting issues raised by the adjustment to the oil-price rise. I shall not resolve them. In each case more research and thought are required. But it might be useful at least to sketch out the issues.

First Issue: Why Did the World Go Into Recession in 1974–5?

The United States and Japan went into severe recession in the early part of 1974 and Western Europe followed later in 1974. Was this the result of the oil-price rise, or rather of deliberate policy?

We have seen that the oil-price rise was certainly deflationary in its impact. One might define the impact deflation as the fall in aggregate demand at a constant interest rate—before extra investment has been induced and, of course, before there has been any autonomous or accommodating fiscal expansion—and also before a multiplier has magnified the original effect. On this basis the initial shocks have been estimated (by two Brookings authors) for the United States and Western Europe as slightly less than 2 per cent of G.N.P. and for Japan about 2·25 per cent. In the case of the estimate for the United States, nearly half of the deflationary impact is attributed to the increase in payments to domestic-oil producers. This assumes that the oil companies' extra profits did not rapidly lead to extra spending—a doubtful assumption. Further, these figures do not take into account the subsequent increase in exports to OPEC countries.

This deflationary effect could have been counteracted. But in fact it was not. In the case of the United States fiscal and monetary policies were both severely restrictive in 1974, and indeed the real stock of money fell sharply. Policy seems to have moved in the opposite direction from that indicated in our earlier model. In Japan also—and indeed more so—monetary and fiscal policies became severely restrictive in 1974. In the case of Western Europe, policies differed somewhat among countries, and the recession generally began later in 1974, but the general tendency was also restrictive, especially in monetary policy. But some countries, notably Britain and Italy, did run large budget deficits in 1974, and in 1975 they were joined in this respect by Germany.

In analysing this experience one could try a number of hypotheses. One possibility is that governments and monetary authorities initially misunderstood the significance of the oil-price rise. They saw it as inflationary rather than deflationary. It is possible that Japanese policy could be interpreted in these terms. Indeed this was not an entirely unreasonable point of view. One could have expected the oil embargo to reduce domestic output significantly, which would then call for a reduction in demand. In fact the fall in output brought about by the embargo was very temporary indeed, and in many countries insignificant. It is also true that an optimal response would have called only for *some* offsetting demand-stimulating measures designed to counteract the deflationary impact of the oil-price rise, but not so much as to return the economies to their original levels of demand. A *net* demand-deflationary effect would remain so as to counteract the cost-inflationary impact of the oil-price rise. But this kind of subtle response calls for an appreciation of the fact that the impact of the oil-price rise was certainly demand-deflationary. It would be difficult to justify deliberate fiscal and monetary contractionary policies because of the oil-price rise.

A second interpretation is that in 1974 the finance ministries and central banks wanted to deflate. They wanted to do so because of the cost inflation—induced by the demand inflation of earlier years—which was already under way. The primary cost inflation created by the oil-price rise, and the secondary cost inflation this was likely to induce as money wages rose to compensate for higher oil prices, strengthened their anti-inflationary resolve. So they welcomed the demand-deflationary impact of the oil-price rise. They understood what it meant and were glad to let it do some of the deflationary work for them that otherwise would have required deliberate and politically difficult policy action. Indeed in some countries, notably the United States and Japan, they supplemented it with such deliberate deflationary-policy actions.

If the second interpretation is correct one can attribute some of the deflation of 1974–5 to the oil-price rise, but cannot really 'blame' the oil-price rise. The deflation was not inevitable, but rather was policy-induced, partly induced by deliberate policy and partly induced by a decision *not* to counteract the deflationary impact of the oil-price rise with stimulating policies. I suspect that there is a lot in this interpretation. But in order to choose between this interpretation and the previous one some research into policy statements, internal Finance Ministry and Central Bank memoranda, and interviews with decision-makers may be necessary.

A third interpretation, but one which does not really exclude the previous one, is that the authorities wanted some deflation, but certainly not as much as they actually got. Nominal demand aggregates tended to rise roughly as expected, but real aggregates fell so much because wages and prices increased much faster than expected and were quite slow to respond to demand deflation. Profits were squeezed and so investment slumped; and later, there was a rise in personal savings as individuals sought to rebuild cash balances and to cover themselves against the uncertainties of the recession. Once this process had got under way there was not a great deal that governments could do to stimulate their economies because of the lags with which demand usually responds. In any case it is clear enough that the eventual fall in actual output relative to potential output in the main countries—notably the United States, Japan, and Germany—was far greater than the initial deflationary impact of the oil-price rise.

Second Issue: Why did International Liquidity Increase, and What Does it Mean?

In 1974 official reserve holdings in the world as a whole rose 19 per cent (by $36 billion). Almost the whole of this increase went to the OPEC countries, so that for the Rest reserves in nominal terms hardly increased (by $3 billion). Since there was a large increase in prices during 1974, especially in the first part of the year, their real reserves declined. Nevertheless, it is of interest how the countries that make up the Rest managed as a group to more than maintain the nominal value of their official reserves while at the same time running a large current-account deficit.

The first answer one might give is that, as already explained, a capital-account surplus offset the current-account deficit. Thus one might say that it was not at all surprising that reserves of the Rest did not change. But this is not a satisfactory answer, since presumably for OPEC the current-account surplus would then be offset by a capital account deficit and one would not expect OPEC to obtain an increase in reserves.

World reserves can increase broadly in three ways. Firstly, there can be an increase in primary reserves, namely gold, SDRs and I.M.F. reserve positions. But there was only a very small increase in these during 1974 ($4 billion), all in reserve positions. Secondly, the reserve currency country—the United States—can run a current account deficit which is financed by other countries accumulating dollars. In that case the Rest obtains liquid assets from the United States in exchange for goods and services. The United States did run a current-account deficit in 1974 ($3·6 billion), but it was quite small in relation to the great increase in nominal reserves. Thirdly, the Rest can obtain dollars by borrowing on the New York and the Euro-dollar markets (or receiving a direct investment inflow). This means, essentially, that the Rest is obtaining liquid assets from the United States and from U.S. and other banks overseas in exchange for incurring somewhat less liquid liabilities. The net asset position of the United States and the Rest does not alter as a result of this, but the composition of assets does. But when the Rest acquires more liquid assets at the cost of incurring less liquid liabilities, it is said that its reserves have increased.

In practice, this is what happened. The Rest paid OPEC for its oil in foreign exchange, i.e. mainly in dollars. Hence OPEC's reserves increased. These were placed either as claims on the United States or as holdings of Euro-dollars—about one-third the former and two-thirds the latter. At this stage one would expect the reserves of the Rest to fall. But then the Rest—or at least some major countries in this group—replenished their reserves by borrowing, mainly in the United States and on the Euro-dollar market. Notably there was public borrowing by France, Italy, and the United Kingdom, and in Japan large borrowing abroad by the commercial banks. This is not the whole story; there were all sorts of flows: Italy borrowed from Germany, there was a short-term revival of sterling as a reserve currency, and so on. But the increase in dollars held outside the United States was the main development.

All this refers to 1974. In 1975 the OPEC current-account

surplus sharply declined (from $65 billion in 1974 to $40 billion in 1975), the combined current-account deficit of the O.E.C.D. countries was even more sharply reduced (from $33 billion to $5·5 billion), and, most relevant here, the increase in world liquidity decelerated (from $36 billion in 1974 to $7·6 billion in 1975). Developing countries—notably Brazil and Mexico—and some Eastern European countries became the main official borrowers on the international private-capital market. But here we are mainly concerned with the year 1974, when the impact of the oil-price rise was clearly felt.

A number of observations can be made about the significance of these developments, and about the way they are described when one uses the usual definitions of reserves and of balance of payments deficits.

Firstly, it is clear that in 1974 the world obtained the reserves it wanted. When there is a well functioning world-capital market— and particularly when the United States has removed controls on capital outflow, as she wisely did early in 1974—and when there is reasonable faith in the dollar, reserves get created as needed. All the endless talk about the need to replace the dollar was shown to be irrelevant. Gold, while still thought of as a reserve asset, could play no part once the gold convertibility of the dollar had ended. SDRs were really irrelevant, other than as new accounting unit. But the world did not wait on endless conferences and meetings to manufacture new reserves—it did not wait until that magic moment when even France would agree to what most other countries wanted. The world market—in which governments were major transactors—brought forth the extra reserves. The dollar has never looked so secure and so useful as a centrepoint of the international monetary system as it did in 1974 and 1975.

Secondly, there is a question of what the significance is of such an increase in reserves as was experienced in 1974, and to a lesser extent, 1975. It is possible that one gives a misleading impression if one simply states that OPEC reserves have increased while the reserves of the Rest have not changed much. The asset positions of many countries in the Rest have certainly deteriorated. Their liquid assets have remained the same as before, but they have increased their less liquid liabilities.

Reserves are designed to allow a country to run a current-account deficit at short notice, perhaps in case of a crisis, whether brought about by a deterioration in the terms of trade, a sudden rise in domestic demand, or anything else. But when there is a well-functioning world capital market, owned reserves are not really needed for this, except in so far as they make or keep a country 'credit-worthy'. The country can always borrow provided it is credit-worthy. Now the question is whether a country such as Britain is less credit-worthy when it has acquired large medium or long-term international liabilities. The answer must be that when these liabilities are backed by substantial increases in domestic assets—as in the case of Britain's North Sea oil—credit-worthiness may not be affected. But when there is no such backing, as in the case of Italy, it may indeed be. Perhaps such a country is somewhat more assured in the short run of being able to finance a current-account deficit when it has an adequate stock of *owned* liquid assets, but in the somewhat longer run the total asset position is likely to become relevant.

Nevertheless, it must be granted that the oil-price rise really presented the world with a very sudden short-term problem. It was undoubtedly an achievement that the system was able to generate the required liquidity in the short run, and so give countries some degree of short-run security about being able to maintain living standards.

Thirdly, there is a fairly subtle issue of whether the increase in liquidity was not generated by a process which simultaneously increased the need for liquidity.

Let us go over the story again. In the first instance dollars were transferred from the Rest to OPEC. So, clearly, OPEC became more liquid and the Rest less liquid. Then the Rest borrowed from the United States, and from the world's international banks, mainly but not wholly American, to replenish official reserves. This meant that official authorities in the Rest, other than the United States, were able to replenish their liquidity. If we combine the OPEC governments and the governments of the Rest, other than the United States government, there was at this stage an increase in liquidity. But at the same time, some institutions became less liquid and so assumed bankers' risk. These institutions were mainly the great international banks, as well as the United States government (and also the German government, when it made a loan to Italy).

In fact, liquidity as a whole in the world did not increase. The risks borne by the banks were, to some extent, spread to their customers and, more important, to the governments that stood behind them as lenders of last resort. In practice, of course, there was a substantial reshuffling of liquidity. The most important banks concerned have been American banks, and behind them—even when these private banks operate in the Euro-dollar market—stands the Federal Reserve. Broadly we can say that for the world as a whole official liquidity has increased and private liquidity has decreased, and that to some extent the risks of higher liquidity in the private sector are borne by governments in the financial centres, especially but not only the United States government.

Third Issue: Was There Need for International Co-ordination of Policies and Current-Account Targets?

When the oil-price rise hit the world economy there was much discussion about the need for international agreements to 'accept the current-account deficits'. There was fear that countries would react to the oil deficits by deflating and imposing trade restrictions, and so plunging the world into depression and trade war in a pointless effort to shift the deficits on to each other. Countries did indeed deflate and plunge the world at least into recession, but it is clear enough that their deflationary policies were *not* mainly motivated by balance-of-payments considerations (with the possible exception of Japan). Furthermore, the major countries in general avoided imposing trade restrictions on any large scale.

Agreement was reached to avoid trade restrictions and to 'accept' the deficits. But it is not so clear what the latter meant. Certainly there was no agreement on a particular pattern of current-account deficits. The general suggestion was that countries should accept their 'oil deficits'—which is what I have called the *primary* deficits. But one cannot say that in any sense countries ended up with their primary deficits. The deficits of Britain and Italy were certainly much greater. On the other hand, Japan managed after a while to get her deficit down below her primary deficit, and Germany had a vast surplus in 1974, though substantially reduced in 1975.

There was much discussion of working out a set of current-account targets, and various suggestions were made as to the appropriate criteria for such targets. The question is whether all this discussion was necessary. The actual balance-of-payments outcome obviously could not wait on agreement on current-account targets. On the other hand, one must concede that the actual outcome may have been influenced by agreement to 'accept' in some sense the deficits. Furthermore, there was agreement to avoid 'competitive devaluations'. The question also arises what that meant in a world where exchange rates were certainly changing and many countries depreciated in relation to the SDR numeraire.

I wish then to ask whether there was need for international agreement of any kind, and what principles governed the actual outcome of current accounts and levels of demand for domestic goods and services in various countries.

A Simple Model of International Adjustment

Let us suppose, to begin with, that the United States is the passive or residual element in the international economy, accepting whatever current account emerges as the result of her own policy of maintaining domestic demand at a desired level and as the result of the exchange-rate policies of other countries. Other countries manage their financial policies so as to attain whatever current accounts they wish, current-account targets being influenced by views about desirable levels of foreign-exchange reserves and willingness to borrow. To the extent that the adverse balance of payments effects of the oil-price rise did not lead countries to borrow in order to sustain reserve levels—as many actually did on a large scale—they would then devalue in relation to the dollar in order to improve their current accounts. Thus they would pay for the restoration of reserve levels in terms of goods and services absorbed by the United States rather than acquisition of illiquid liabilities. At the same time each could use its financial (fiscal, monetary, and exchange-rate) policies to manage its domestic economy as it wished.

When the exchange rate is an instrument of policy a country has at least two instruments of policy, and so should be able to attain the two targets of internal and external balance. Furthermore, every country (other than the United States) can get the current account it wants. If its government wishes to borrow for consumption maintenance, as did Britain's or Italy's, then that is its choice; and similarly, if a country wishes to cut its deficit drastically, like Japan, then that also is an acceptable choice. In the world of flexible exchange rates countries are able to insulate themselves from other countries' inflation. As will be discussed in Chapter 11, they are not able to insulate themselves from all *real* changes abroad, including the real output effects of foreign deflation, but countries do have a degree of freedom, so that one is not justified in blaming a domestic deflation or inflation on foreigners. Given a willingness to accept consequences, there is no need to wait for an American or a German boom before inflating the British economy, if that is what the British government really wanted.

A World of Rigid Real Exchange Rates

To some extent this is what actually happened. Exchange rates did alter and countries had widely varying demand policies. Nevertheless, countries were not as free as this approach suggests. The constraint was not on levels of current deficits and surpluses. There can hardly have been such constraints when Germany managed to run a $9.8 billion surplus and the United Kingdom a $8.5 billion deficit in 1974, and Japan managed to turn a $5.7 billion deficit in the first half of 1974 into a $1 billion surplus in the second half. The constraint was rather on real exchange rates—that is, on movements of exchange rates that effectively altered competitiveness.

The fear that countries had about each other's policies was not that their neighbours would run surpluses, but rather that their neighbours' export industries could outcompete the home industries, this competition being aided by 'unfair' exchange-rate movements designed to reduce or eliminate the neighbour's deficits. In terms of my classification earlier, changes in competitiveness would give rise to *tertiary* imbalances, and in general such tertiary imbalances were avoided. One could argue that there was at least implicit international agreement to avoid such changes. This meant that, in a sense, we were back in a world of fixed exchange rates, but fixed *real* rates, not fixed nominal ones.

In such a world of relatively rigid real rates there could still be a variety of outcomes for current accounts—as indeed there was. The outcomes depended on the sizes of the primary and secondary deficits, and on each country's aggregate demand policies (differences here yielding the quaternary imbalances). A country that wanted to maintain a high level of domestic demand would have to accept a larger current deficit, and would feel justified in urging other countries to expand demand more so as to counteract this. In other words, we are back in a familiar world of one instrument and two targets. It is in this world with relatively rigid real exchange rates that one can understand the concern about international co-ordination of demand policies.

What was the reason for this rigidity of real exchange rates? Why was there reluctance to approve of other countries' exchange depreciations that did more than compensate for their rises in domestic money costs? One might argue that if Japan depreciates so much as to lower her real exchange rate, and allow her motor-car industry to outcompete that of Britain, then Britain could maintain her total level of demand for domestically produced goods and services by expansionary fiscal or perhaps monetary policy that compensates for the reduced competitiveness of foreign-traded goods. Thus Britain could allow Japan her desired improvement in the current balance while maintaining full employment in Britain.

But this is looking at the problem in excessively aggregative terms. The reason for the rigidity of real exchange rates was concern for the interests of import-competing and export industries. The beneficiaries of the extra domestic demand would be mainly the sectors producing non-traded goods and services, since extra demand for traded goods would spill abroad. In the short run resources are not readily mobile between the traded and non-traded sectors. Hence unemployment in Britain's export and import-competing industries would be likely when Japan became more competitive. Even if resources were mobile—so that full employment could be maintained—a redistribution of domestic incomes away from the traded-goods sectors towards the non-traded-goods sectors would be inevitable. And this redistribution is generally not desired. Furthermore, such declines in competitiveness of traded-goods industries create great pressures for trade restrictions. Hence there is an implicit agreement to avoid substantial changes in competitiveness.

If countries had felt free to alter exchange rates and domestic monetary and fiscal policies as they wished, and their balance-of-payments policies had been directed to attaining certain levels of current accounts or reserves, or perhaps if they had specific exchange-rate objectives, the question would arise as to the freedom of the United States. Must the United States be passive and unable to influence current-account and exchange-rate outcomes? I shall return to this question in Chapter 12.

REFERENCES

Background for this chapter comes from various issues of O.E.C.D., *Economic Outlook*, the *Annual Report of 1975* of the International Monetary Fund, and the 46th *Annual Report* of the Bank for International Settlements, these three regular publications being in fact the best sources for information on developments in the international monetary field. Figures come from *International Financial Statistics*.

Discussions of current account targets and the need to allocate the 'oil deficit' were common in 1974 and early 1975. See R. Solomon, 'The Allocation of Oil Deficits', *Brookings Papers on Economic Activity*, 1975 (1), 61–79, Andrew D. Crockett and Duncan Ripley, 'Sharing the Oil Deficit', *Staff Papers*, 22 (July 1975), 284–312, and John Williamson's contribution to Edward R. Fried and Charles L. Schultze (eds.), *Higher Oil Prices and the World Economy*, Brookings Institution, Washington, 1975.

MONETARY INTEGRATION
IN EUROPE

10

EUROPEAN MONETARY INTEGRATION: THE MAIN ISSUES

IN this chapter I shall look at the European monetary-integration issue. I shall briefly examine the arguments for and against, taking into account developments since the great inflation of 1972–3. I shall then look at the European Monetary System which was established in 1979 and ask to what extent it can be regarded as a movement towards integration.

Background

Let me begin with a brief review of the main concepts and events. Monetary integration can be regarded as having two components, namely exchange-rate union and capital-market integration. Since the world capital market is in any case highly integrated now while, by contrast, we are certainly not in a world of fixed exchange rates, the important aspect of the European monetary integration proposal that was put forward in 1970 is that the European Community shall become an area within which exchange rates are fixed. This means, for example, that the franc–D-mark rate would be fixed, even though the two rates together could still alter relative to outside currencies, such as the dollar. I am not dismissing the importance of capital market integration when I focus on exchange-rate union. There are extensive national controls on capital movements within the Community and laws affecting investment are not harmonized. Nevertheless, I think it can be argued that a considerable degree of capital-market integration—that is freedom of capital movements and remittances—does exist, partly because various controls and attempts to separate markets are not really very effective.

One should also make a distinction between a *pseudo* exchange-rate union and a *complete* exchange-rate union. In the pseudo-union the various member countries still have their own central banks and foreign-exchange reserves, and hence still determine their own money supply or credit policies. But they agree to manage their policies so as to maintain fixed-exchange-rate relationships. There may also be some arrangements where surplus countries provide limited financing for deficit countries. By contrast, in a complete exchange-rate union, foreign-exchange reserves are pooled and there is a central monetary authority. Hence there is a complete assurance that the fixed-exchange-rate relationships will be maintained. Most people would regard the latter, and not the former, as representing monetary integration proper. But the pseudo-union nevertheless needs to be looked at because most proposals for European monetary integration involve going through a pseudo-union stage, because sometimes indeed the pseudo-union is mistaken for the real thing, and because particular problems arise with the pseudo-union that would not arise with a complete union.

The initiative for European monetary integration was political rather than economic. It cannot be said that there was a felt economic need; rather there was a felt political need to keep the movement towards European integration going once the industrial customs union and the common agricultural policy had been achieved. Out of this came the Werner Report of October, 1970. This report proposed the establishment in stages of an economic and monetary union by 1980. There was to be a single Community currency by then or, alternatively, the rigid fixing of exchange rates with complete elimination of margins of fluctuations and the total and irreversible interconvertibility of such currencies; and in addition complete liberalization of all capital movements within the area and a common central banking system. The first stage was to involve the narrowing of exchange margins.

It came to be realized that the Werner proposals were unrealistic. I shall not tell the long, elaborate story of numerous conferences and decisions, of how some exchange margins were indeed narrowed from April 1972 as part of the 'snake-in-the-tunnel' scheme, but at various times countries left the scheme and allowed their currencies to depreciate, and especially of how the succession of international monetary crises and upheavals in 1971 and since got in the way of a steady step-by-step progression towards monetary integration. The narrow-margins arrangement or 'snake' meant that the monetary authorities of a number of countries intervened in the markets so as to keep the exchange margins relative to each other within certain limits. At the same time the 'snake' as a whole was allowed to fluctuate relative to outside currencies, that is, especially the dollar. The centre of the snake system was the D-Mark. At certain times France, Italy, and Britain were in the system, but when they were unable to maintain their rates, they withdrew and depreciated. In 1979 the European Monetary System (E.M.S.) was established. It was essentially a development of the snake, and I shall discuss it later.

The Usual Arguments

While the main motive for the proposals for monetary-integration was political, other arguments in favour can be made. A strong argument from the point of view of the European integrationists is that fiscal integration would certainly be very difficult without a complete exchange-rate union. Most people have naturally seen some degree of fiscal integration as an inevitable feature of progress towards European union. Furthermore, it was thought that trade and capital movements within the area would be made easier by having firmly fixed exchange rates, one money being more efficient than several moneys. In addition, many people thought that an exchange-rate union was the way to avoid the endless, irritating, and—to politicians—puzzling exchange crises which had bedevilled the international monetary system.

On this latter point, it is clear that if the exchange rates are irrevocably fixed, there will be no speculative capital movements within the area. Indeed, if there is only one money there cannot be movements from one money to another. But this undoubted benefit would result only from a *complete* exchange-rate union. It can be argued that a *pseudo*-union—which restores the Bretton Woods system of 'fixed but adjustable' rates within the integrated area—is *more* conducive to destabilizing private speculation than a system of freely floating rates or a system where, at least, there is no 'firm but revocable' commitment by the monetary authorities to particular rates.

The main argument against monetary integration has been the following: If a country wants to maintain both internal and external balance it needs two instruments of policy. If the exchange-rate instrument is no longer available to it, demand-management policy

would need to be assigned to the external-balance target. Some
countries would then end up with more unemployment than they
wanted and others with more inflation. The more the short-term
'Phillips curves' of the member countries differed and monetary
authorities' views about the optimal points on these curves diverged,
the greater this problem would be. But even if the member
countries' desired rates of inflation happened to be about the same,
there might still be some need for changes in exchange-rate
relationships because of structural changes, demand shifts, and so
on.

The argument follows from the basic model which was expounded
in Chapter 1 and which I have used many times since. It involves
several assumptions. The main assumption is that money wages (or
prices of non-traded goods) are either rigid downwards or depend on
some kind of 'Phillips curve' function. It hinges on the view that the
exchange rate has a crucial role as a switching device. Naturally, if
one accepts this model one must conclude that if a country loses the
exchange rate as an instrument of policy it will incur a cost, the cost
of 'departure from internal balance'.

It is not difficult to show that, given these assumptions, neither
mobility of capital, nor regional policy, nor labour mobility are
likely to solve the problems created by fixity of exchange rates.
Capital mobility is concerned with financing, but the problem is one
of adjustment. If Italy's real-wage rates are too high, and a demand-
management policy which aims at full employment then leads to a
balance-of-payments deficit, foreign borrowing facilitated by capital
mobility can indeed allow this situation to continue for some time—
it can allow workers' consumption to continue at original levels—
but it will not provide an inducement or mechanism for bringing
real wages down and so adjusting them to a new situation. It can
only finance a holding operation or deal with temporary dis-
equilibria. Community regional policy involves subsidization through
the fiscal system, and while it can be used to some extent to
encourage adjustment, it is really a form of foreign aid—and thus,
again, essentially it is a form of financing. Labour mobility can be
helpful, but the fact is that there is just not enough mobility between
the various members of the E.E.C. for governments to feel that they
can rely on this as the main method of adjustment. Furthermore,
even if unemployment induced by a contractionary demand policy
does lead to out-migration in time, governments are not likely to

welcome this particular solution even though it does help to solve an unemployment problem.

This argument against monetary-integration has been widely accepted, especially in the larger countries of the E.E.C. It has certainly been accepted in Britain. The advocates of continued British membership of the E.E.C., who won the referendum in 1975 by a wide margin, never subscribed to the objective of 'economic and monetary union'. They made it clear that it was a long-term objective not to be taken seriously within the forseeable future. As for the French, it has been apparent that, while they have often been advocates of fixed rates and have been strong supporters of the monetary integration objective, they have never hesitated to devalue the franc in relation to other E.E.C. currencies when their government has thought it necessary for the sake of maintaining French employment and foreign-exchange reserves. Furthermore, France has never accepted the idea of a firm central political control. Yet complete monetary integration requires a single central bank, and surely a single central bank for the E.E.C. requires some kind of firm central political control.

How the Events of 1973 to 1975 Affected the Situation

The events of 1973 to 1975 affected this issue in two ways. Firstly, the great inflation blew apart the 'expectations-augmented' short-run Phillips curve of various countries. This meant that (to use the concept of Chapter 4) the 'desired' inflation rates of various countries greatly diverged, and hence great costs would have been imposed if inflation rates had been forced together by exchange-rate union. For this reason any concerted movement towards exchange-rate union came to a dead stop in 1974. This was dramatized by the departure of France from the snake.

Once a world inflation had got going, and the initial policy reactions differed between countries, it was inevitable that rates of inflation would diverge—unless indeed countries with the high inflation rates were willing to accept sudden and large unemployment as the cost of getting back to equilibrium. Nominal exchange rates thus had to diverge sharply so as to avoid excessive divergences in real exchange rates. For this reason the events of 1974 and 1975 put a stop to any concerted progress towards monetary integration. The standard argument against monetary integration certainly appeared to apply to the short-run situation.

But there is a second implication of events since 1974. In a fundamental sense the argument against monetary integration has been weakened. One can interpret events as showing that monetary expansion can only increase employment in the short-run. And expansion now is at the inevitable cost of reducing employment later as the authorities try to put an end to an accelerating rate of inflation. If one accepts this Friedmanite view one should conclude that once the various members of the European Community have restored monetary equilibrium they should pursue a policy of stable monetary growth and give up monetary policy as a short-term employment-stabilizing device. And in that case they might as well fix their nominal exchange rates relative to each other, so avoiding short-term real exchange-rate instability owing to capital movements.

European Monetary System

The European Monetary System was established in 1979 as a result of initiatives from the German Chancellor and the French President. Essentially it represents a strengthening and enlargement of the 'snake', with France and Italy included.

The arrangements are complicated, but the E.M.S. has three key features. Firstly, a bilateral exchange-rate grid—i.e. a set of central, bilateral rates—has been established. The permissible margin of fluctuations on either side of a central rate is 2.25 per cent, except in the case of Italy, where it is 6 per cent. For each bilateral rate, the relevant two central banks have to intervene to an unlimited extent to keep the rate within the margins, buying and selling each other's currency. Thus the aim is to maintain short-term bilateral exchange-rate stability. The idea is basically the same as in the case of the snake, reflecting a dislike of floating exchange rates. Secondly, there are much-extended credit facilities, both short term and medium term. Short-term credits are unconditional, while policy conditions are attached to medium-term credits. In this respect the system differs significantly from the previous arrangements. The credibility of existing rates is greatly strengthened when the available financial resources are so much greater. Thirdly, there is no irrevocable commitment to the central rates. It is quite clear that, as in the snake, they can be changed after appropriate discussions. One view is that they should be changed readily to avoid the build-up of speculative pressures.

Thus the E.M.S. is not even a pseudo-union. It is best described as a system of reluctant bilateral exchange-rate adjustment. The proclaimed philosophy behind the E.M.S. is the same as that behind a pseudo-union: countries' monetary policies should be adapted to maintain exchange-rate stability—at least over the medium-term, since credit facilities can cope with the short-term. But there is no element of compulsion and, in the case of the E.M.S., not even a firm commitment. The establishment of the E.M.S. reflected a dissatisfaction with exchange-rate instability and also with large real exchange-rate changes, like those associated with the depreciation of the dollar from 1976 to 1978.

By 1984 it was possible to assess the workings of the system and to ask whether it could be regarded as at least a movement towards monetary integration. The central issue has always been that German inflation rates have been much less than the French and Italian ones. This meant that nominal rates had to be adjusted at intervals, or alternatively real exchange rates had to be allowed to get out of line, leading to strains on competitive situations.

Over the period from 1979 to 1984 there were five realignments of exchange rates. The Lira depreciated relative to the D-mark by about 27 per cent over the whole period, and this roughly compensated for the inflation differential. The French franc depreciated relative to the D-Mark by at least 20 per cent. Most of the realignments were individually quite small, except for the March 1983 one, which followed French and German elections. At that time the Lira and French franc depreciated over 8 per cent relative to the D-Mark.

There have been two periods of nominal-rate stability. The first was at the beginning, up to October 1981, and the second since March 1983. In the first period there were very large inflation differentials: 1980 to 1981 German inflation averaged 4.5 per cent, French inflation 11.3 per cent, and Italian inflation 19.2 per cent. In the second period they were still large, but at least declining. Hence real rates diverged greatly.

One can only understand what happened within the E.M.S. if one understands the special role of the D-Mark in relation to the U.S. dollar. When there are capital movements out of the United States they tend to go into the D-Mark rather than the other E.M.S.

currencies, so that the D-Mark appreciates not only relative to the dollar but also relative to the other currencies. This puts great strains on the system, since, because of the inflation differentials, the natural tendency is for the D-Mark to appreciate in any case. On the other hand, appreciation of the dollar helps the system by keeping the D-Mark relatively low. For much of the time that the E.M.S. existed the dollar was appreciating, so this helped the system greatly. The only exception was a period in late 1982 when it depreciated, which immediately put a strain on the system.

There is some evidence that nominal exchange rate variability within the E.M.S. has been less than for the same currencies before the E.M.S. or for the major floating rates outside the system (dollar, yen, sterling) over the same period. It is quite clear, and indeed an inevitable feature of the system, that it has protected the exchange-rate relationships of the member currencies from *short-term* volatility of the kind that their rates experience relative to the dollar. This is perhaps its main result.

The E.M.S. has clearly failed to bring about close convergence of policies or of inflation rates. Whether there has been at least a tendency to policy convergence because of the E.M.S. is more difficult to answer. Since 1983, and perhaps earlier, there has been such a tendency, but it has to be remembered that the monetary (though not fiscal) policies of the United States, Japan, Canada, Britain, and Germany have all converged in an anti-inflationary direction, and it is not surprising that the other E.M.S. countries have tended to follow, even though Italy has been rather a laggard and France was temporarily the odd-man-out. On the other hand one could well conclude that French restrictionist policies, which followed her short-lived expansionist experiment after the election of the Mitterand government, were encouraged by the obligation to avoid excessive devaluation of the franc within the system, and to that extent policy convergence between France and Germany can be attributed to membership of the system.

To summarize, the E.M.S. can be regarded as a hesitant step towards monetary integration but is still nowhere near a pseudo-union. It provides at least a framework for further movement, and possibly imposed some anti-inflationary pressures on France and Italy, countries that can usually benefit from such pressures.

REFERENCES

The theory of monetary integration and the main issues are set out in W. M. Corden, *Monetary Integration*, Essays in International Finance No. 93, Princeton, 1972. Another theoretical exposition, essentially along Keynesian lines, and using the Phillips-curve concept, is in J. Marcus Fleming, 'On Exchange Rate Unification', *Economic Journal*, 81 (September 1971), 467–88. Many issues of European monetary integration are discussed in Laurence Krause and Walter Salant (eds.), *European Monetary Unification and its Meaning for the United States*, The Brookings Institution, Washington, 1973, a very comprehensive book on the subject.

Relevant reports dealing with paths to European monetary integration are *Report to the Council and the Commission on the Realisation by Stages of Economic and Monetary Union in the European Communities* (Werner Report), Commission of the European Communities, Brussels, 1970; Study Group on Economic and Monetary Union, *European Economic Integration and Monetary Unification*, Document II/520/1/73–E, Commission of the European Communities, Brussels, 1973; Report of the Study Group, *Economic and Monetary Union 1980*, Document II/675/3/74, Commission of the European Communities, Brussels, 1975; and Leo Tindemans, 'European Union', *Bulletin of the European Communities*, Supplement, 1, 1976 (Tindemans Report).

The complicated arrangements of the European Monetary System are explained in the 49th *Annual Report* of the Bank for International Settlements, pp. 144–8, and every year the *Annual Report* of the B.I.S. contains an account of E.M.S. developments, with substantial reviews in the 52nd and 53rd *Reports* (1982 and 1983), on which I have drawn here. See also Tommaso Padoa-Schioppa, 'The European Monetary System After Five Years', in W. H. Buiter and R. C. Marston (eds.), *International Economic Policy Coordination*, Cambridge University Press, Cambridge, 1985. This paper provides support for the view that the E.M.S. has made the bilateral nominal rates more stable.

THE WORLD OF FLEXIBLE EXCHANGE RATES
AND CAPITAL MOBILITY

11

THE INTERNATIONAL TRANSMISSION OF DISTURBANCES

IN the flexible exchange-rate regime every country can choose its own inflation rate without undesired balance-of-payments surpluses or deficits and without facing problems of sterilization. In other words, countries can have monetary independence. This conclusion follows from the earlier analysis in this book and is well-known. But this does not mean that disturbances—even monetary disturbances —are not transmitted between countries. Events since 1974 have certainly borne this out. In a world of flexible exchange rates there are still *real* links between countries, the mechanisms of the transmission being (1) the terms of trade and (2) the capital market. For example, a monetary disturbance in one country will have effects on output in that country—and thus have *real* and not just nominal effects—and this, in turn, may affect the terms of trade, and thus have real effects on another country. In turn, the other country's monetary policy stance, while independent in principle, may respond to the change in its terms of trade.

The purpose of this chapter is to present a systematic analysis of the transmission of policy disturbances from one large country (the United States) to other countries (represented here by Germany) when the exchange rate is floating. Short-term expectational effects on the exchange rate will generally be ignored, but the analysis is short-term in the sense that it allows for Keynesian effects of demand on output. Disturbances resulting from expectations of policy changes are continuous and very important, especially in explaining short-term fluctuations in the exchange rate. They tend to have effects in the same direction as the actual policy changes. Here I assume that these policy changes are not fully expected before they actually happen, which would be broadly true in most cases.

It is common to analyse the effects of a monetary policy change—for example, an open-market operation that expands the money supply—while holding fiscal policy constant, or alternatively to analyse a fiscal policy change—for example, an increase in government expenditure that leads to a bond-financed budget deficit—while holding the money supply constant. Considering such a policy change in the United States, in each case there are two mechanisms of transmission to Germany. The first operates via the real output effects in the United States and then the terms of trade, and it operates even when there are no effects through the capital market. It will be called the 'locomotive effect' for reasons to be given later. The second operates through the capital account—and hence through current-account imbalance—and thus depends crucially on the international mobility of capital. This second transmission mechanism will also affect the terms of trade, but it does not necessarily require monetary or fiscal policy changes to affect aggregate real output in the United States. Hence it is not dependent on Keynesian effects in the United States.

Here I intend to separate the two transmission mechanisms very carefully, though bringing them together at the end. Rather than first tracing out the effects on Germany of a U.S. monetary expansion and then of a U.S. fiscal expansion, I shall consider two policy mixes: one policy mix isolates the transmission process through real output and the terms of trade, while the other mix isolates the transmission process through the capital market. In each case I shall consider not just the original policies in the United States, their effects in the United States, and then the transmission processes, but also the market and policy reactions in Germany. Theoretical analysis of the capital market transmission has been dominated by the Mundell–Fleming model. But it will be shown that this makes very special assumptions, especially about the policy reactions. Therefore I shall certainly have to go beyond this influential model.

Positive Transmission through the Terms of Trade

A monetary expansion tends to lower the interest rate and a fiscal expansion to raise it. Let us now assume that there is a combination of monetary and fiscal expansion in the United States that keeps the interest rate unchanged before any capital moves, so that there is, in fact, no incentive for any capital inflow or outflow (I assume that there are no net capital movements initially). In this way we are able to eliminate capital-market effects of the two policies and focus on the direct expansionary effects of the increase in aggregate demand. The current account will have to stay in balance.

I shall now assume that a U.S. demand expansion raises real output and hence real incomes in the United States. At a constant exchange rate some part of the extra incomes would be spent on German goods, and therefore the U.S. balance of payments would deteriorate. Hence the dollar has to depreciate. The expansion is likely to increase U.S. inflation, so—if the German rate of inflation stays constant—the dollar would certainly have to depreciate in nominal terms sufficiently at the minimum to maintain a constant real exchange rate (maintain purchasing-power parity). But, in fact, it would have to depreciate more—that is, to depreciate in *real* terms—in order to switch expenditure away from German goods on to U.S. goods and thus maintain current-account balance. At this point it should be noted that the depreciation is likely to lower real wages in the United States, other things being equal. I am assuming that any rise in nominal wages will lag behind the rise in prices, so that there is not complete real-wage rigidity.

The net result will be to worsen the U.S. and improve the German terms of trade. From a world-market point of view the essential point is that the output of U.S. goods has risen but, at constant prices, demand for U.S. goods has risen by less, since some of the extra demand generated by the higher income is spent on German goods. The terms-of-trade change is then required to restore equilibrium.

This improvement in the German terms of trade will have repercussions in Germany. It would tend to raise real wages. If the real wage is fixed in terms of Germany's own products, a rise in real wages from the point of view of German workers as consumers is inevitable as a result of the fall in the relative price of imports from the United States. Such a rise in real wages is a favourable transmission, even though employment in Germany will be constant if the real wage in terms of Germany's own products stays fixed (assuming productivity is constant).

The important further development of the argument is that there may well be an employment response in Germany. One might first consider the extreme case of real-wage rigidity. Suppose that the trade unions in Germany ensured that the *income* real wage in Germany stayed constant, at least after a short adjustment lag. This would mean that a decline in the relative price of imports would lead to a reduction in the real wage in terms of Germany's own products, and hence to an increase in employment. In a more dynamic context, there may be a continual rise in nominal wages and prices, and the rise in nominal wages will be moderated when import prices decline, or rise less than before, owing to the improvement in the terms of trade. In any case, while some of the improvement in the terms of trade may be taken out in higher (income) real wages, some part may be taken out in lower product real wages, and hence in greater employment and German output.

The economic expansion in the United States has then had a *positive transmission* effect in Germany. In so far as it does so it will itself affect the terms of trade. Greater German output will tend to worsen the German terms of trade and so moderate the initial terms-of-trade improvement. This will moderate both the rise in real wages in Germany and the decline in real wages in the United States.

The Locomotive Theory

During the recession of 1975 to 1978 a so-called 'locomotive theory' was sponsored by O.E.C.D. and by some U.S. officials which argued that expansion in one country depended to some extent on expansion by others. In particular, Germany and Japan were urged to stimulate their economies so as to allow economic recovery elsewhere. When the United States did embark on a prolonged expansion it was argued that she was doing duty as a 'locomotive' for the rest of the world. A first reaction might be that this view was based on fixed exchange-rate thinking even though exchange rates between the major countries were either floating or, at least, were by no means firmly fixed. But the preceding analysis provides some rationale for the locomotive theory. While a country is free to stimulate its economy by some combination of monetary and fiscal policy, and flexible rates give it monetary-policy freedom, even with flexible rates countries can influence each others' macroeconomic constraints.

The main argument can be put as follows: a unilateral expansion by Germany would lead to D-Mark depreciation, worsening Germany's terms of trade and lowering her real wage rates. The attempt by German wage-earners to restore their real wages would then set up an inflationary process which would eventually force a reversal of the original expansion. But if other countries expanded at the same time, raising demand for German goods, the initial German depreciation could be avoided, and hence the German terms of trade would not need to fall. Sustained joint expansion is then possible; unilateral expansion is not. In terms of an O.E.C.D. concept which followed the locomotive theory, countries need to move 'in convoy.'

The argument can also be put in Phillips-curve terms. Economic expansion by the United States will shift the German Phillips curve in a favourable direction. While Germany *could* choose any point on its curve, it will find it optimal to choose a point with less unemployment than before because it will now be possible to combine this with a lower inflation rate. Economic expansion in the United States will then have encouraged expansion in Germany. Expansion in Germany would have been possible without U.S. expansion—since Germany is assumed to have monetary independence—but at greater cost in terms of inflation.

The mechanism by which expansion in one country affects another country's Phillips curve favourably is through the terms of trade. If U.S. expansion improves the German terms of trade through raising demand for German exports, if a terms of trade improvement raises the real wage compatible with a given level of employment, and if, in addition, the Phillips curve reflects the dynamic process of reducing the real wage (and hence raising employment) through unanticipated inflation, then a U.S. expansion will have such a favourable Phillips-curve effect in Germany.

It has to be underlined that a crucial assumption in this argument is that a nominal expansion in the United States *can* have real effects, at least in the short run. But it is possible that the short-run is so brief that a short-run expansion is hardly worth while once the effects on inflationary expectations are taken into account. The evidence from the United States in the Carter period shows that it is possible to obtain big increases in output as a result of demand expansionary policies, but that, after a lag, there are inflationary effects that force a reversal of policies. Similarly, the monetary policy-induced recession of 1980–2 shows that contractionary demand policies can have severe real effects, but that, after a lag, the rate of inflation will decline, in that case quite drastically. In other words, the evidence shows that in the United States there is something like a non-vertical short-term Phillips curve, and that the short term is long enough to be very noticeable. The extreme predictions of some rational-expectations theorists have not been borne out.

Negative Transmission

Some qualifications to the simple argument presented above must now be noted. Positive transmission is not inevitable. Germany may *not* benefit from a U.S. expansion. These qualifications do not necessarily destroy the argument, but they do modify it, and in certain circumstances may indeed reverse it.

Firstly, a U.S. expansion may not worsen her terms of trade. One can envisage the following case, admittedly somewhat theoretical. A U.S. expansion raises the average price-level relative to the level of nominal wages and so lowers the real wage. But import-competing goods are labour-intensive while exportables are capital- or natural-resource-intensive. With lower real wages the relative price of the latter category of products then rises. In terms of Harry Johnson's concepts, the U.S. economic expansion is *anti-trade biased*, expanding the output of importables relative to exportables, and so possibly improving the U.S. terms of trade.

But this is not a very realistic case. It is more realistic to think in terms of a world of more than two countries. If two of these countries are competitive rather than complementary in world markets—for example as buyers of raw materials—the expansion of one may worsen the terms of trade of the other. There is then *negative transmission*.

The mechanism of such negative transmission is simple. A U.S. expansion raises demand for commodities which Germany imports. Given that commodity prices are more flexible than prices of manufactures, the terms of trade then turn against both countries, and in favour of commodity exporters. It is possible, for example, that the U.S. expansions of 1972–3 and 1977–8 turned the world oil-market into a sellers' market and so contributed to the two oil shocks, which certainly had adverse effects on the Phillips curves of other oil-importing countries. When effects on world commodity markets are taken into account it is by no means certain that smaller industrial countries benefit when the United States, Japan, and

Germany expand. While there is still positive transmission to exporters of primary commodities there is negative transmission to commodity importers.

A second qualification is that, even if the German terms of trade do improve, this may not shift the German Phillips curve in a favourable direction. In fact, for Germany and other industrial countries it is plausible that a terms-of-trade improvement tends to raise real wages for given employment and so shifts the Phillips curve favourably. But in the case of a primary-product exporting country the link between the terms of trade and the Phillips curve may go the other way: a rise in relative food or raw-material prices may tend to lower real wages for a given employment level.

A final qualification is that Germany will need to take into account the longer-term effects of a U.S. expansion. Suppose that the U.S. engaged in a demand expansion which has the immediate and welcome effect of expanding U.S. output, improving the German terms of trade, and so permitting some German expansion. But at the same time the U.S. expansion stimulates inflationary expectations, and possibly even an immediate rise in the rate of inflation. This need not have any immediate adverse effect on Germany, since she can always insulate herself from U.S. inflation by appreciation of the D-Mark. The favourable *real* effect of the U.S. expansion spills over into Germany but the unfavourable *nominal* effect does not. It would thus seem that it is always in Germany's interest to encourage U.S. expansion, and vice versa.

The qualification is that, in due course, the acceleration of inflation in the United States would have unfavourable *real* effects. If it were not expected to have such adverse real effects, but were only expected to have nominal effects, it would be hard to see why the United States and other countries trade-off higher current expansion against higher inflation. In due course the increased U.S. inflation would either have adverse effects on productivity or, more likely, bring forth counteracting deflationary demand policies to end the inflation. The resulting recession would then worsen the terms of trade of Germany.

It follows that a U.S. expansion today may have a positive transmission effect on Germany today, allowing her to expand without more inflation, and possibly even with less, but may have a negative effect some years later. In a *total* sense Germany could lose from a current U.S. expansion, depending on a whole lot of considerations, including the extent to which she discounts the future.

Capital Market Transmission

I now turn to the international transmission of disturbances through the capital market. I propose to eliminate the 'locomotive' considerations just discussed by assuming that employment and aggregate output in the United States stay constant. We can imagine a bond-financed fiscal expansion combined with a monetary contraction such that demand for U.S.-produced goods stays constant.

The fiscal expansion raises the U.S. interest rate (before international capital mobility comes into play) and *raises* the demand for U.S. goods, while the monetary contraction further raises the interest rate and *lowers* aggregate demand. Alternatively, instead of operating in a Keynesian framework and assuming a monetary policy that maintains demand constant for any given fiscal expansion, we could make the 'new classical' assumption that price and wage flexibility maintain a constant or 'natural' level of employment. That could be an appropriate assumption for a medium-term analysis of a fiscal expansion which is expected to be prolonged, such as the U.S. fiscal expansion which began in 1982. Incidentally, I am making the normal assumption here that the U.S. fiscal expansion will not lead directly to extra private savings in the United States that are sufficient to finance the deficit. If there were this private savings reaction an increase in government expenditure that was bond-financed would not have the net effect of raising the demand for goods, and so would not be expansionary. Nor would it raise the interest rate. It is a theme of recent theoretical work (the *Ricardian theorem*) that there may be at least some tendency to such an offsetting rise in savings as taxpayers foresee the increase in the future tax burden to meet government interest payments.

At this stage, before capital flows into the United States as a result of the higher interest rate, the U.S. current account is still in balance. The budget deficit is offset by the crowding-out of private investment that has resulted from the higher interest rate. Thus the flow of U.S. private savings that previously financed U.S. private investment now finances the budget deficit. In addition, it could be financed by some increase in savings for the 'Ricardian' reasons just mentioned. We can then imagine that, after a lag, the higher interest rate leads to capital inflow and appreciation of the dollar. As it does so the interest rate will fall towards the German interest rate, and private investment will recover. A U.S. current-account deficit which is equal to the budget deficit, less the remaining decline in private investment, will emerge. Essentially the budget deficit is financed both by German savings and by a diversion of U.S. savings away from U.S. investment, and, in addition, it may be financed by some rise in U.S. savings.

The extent of the dollar appreciation and the decline of the interest rate towards the German interest rate will depend both on the degree of substitutability of U.S. and German financial assets and on the German policy reaction. Here it can be realistically assumed that the U.S. interest rate will finally be higher than it was initially, even though it will be lower than if capital had not been internationally mobile at all. It also seems reasonable to assume that the dollar must appreciate—and the evidence is pretty clear here—but there is a portfolio effect making for depreciation. The U.S. Treasury is supplying more and more dollar-denominated bonds, while the extra demand for bonds (resulting from the crowding out of investment in both countries) may to some extent be for D-Mark-denominated bonds.

There are various implications of the budget deficit for the United States, notably the continuous increase in her public debt, the growth-retarding effect of lower domestic private investment, and the adverse effects on tradable-goods industries resulting from the real appreciation, the last, in turn, leading to intensified protectionist pressures. A favourable effect for the United States is the improvement in her terms of trade, and there may also be favourable effects of the extra government expenditures and the tax cuts that gave rise to the budget deficit. But here I am concerned primarily with the effects on Germany, to which I now turn.

In Germany everything hinges on the labour market and policy reactions. Let us assume that the nominal wage (or its rate of increase) is given, that the real wage is flexible, and that, as in the United States, monetary policy is adjusted so as to maintain constant overall employment. These are only initial assumptions and must certainly be varied later. Let us also assume as a starting point that capital mobility between the United States and Germany is perfect and that U.S. and German bonds are perfect substitutes.

The world rate of interest will then rise compared to the initial position, the dollar real exchange rate will appreciate and hence the D-Mark real rate will depreciate, profitability of tradable-goods industries in the United States will decline and in Germany rise, and the reverse with regard to the non-tradable industries. The U.S. fiscal deficit will be partly financed by a decline in German domestic investment resulting from the higher interest rate—German savers exporting a part of their savings. There will be a continuous portfolio adjustment as the U.S. government absorbs more and more of the world's savings; hence one should not expect the world interest rate, nor the exchange rate, to stabilize even if the budget deficit is a stable flow for some time. But the general direction of movement is clear. The various capital-market effects will be modified the less is the substitutability of U.S. for German bonds and the less mobile is capital, possibly because of exchange controls.

An important aspect is the effect on German real wages. Real wages are likely to fall as a result of the D-Mark depreciation, and especially as a result of the probable terms-of-trade deterioration. There has been an increase in U.S. expenditure and a decline in German expenditure, and this is likely to shift the pattern of world demand towards U.S. goods, and so improve the U.S. terms of trade. On the other hand, if wages are not uniform in the economy, wage-earners in tradable-goods industries may gain. If Germany is a net creditor at floating or variable interest rates, as a nation she may benefit from the higher world interest rate—that is, from the opportunity to invest more profitably in the United States—and these benefits may filter down to her wage-earners in so far as they are also savers and, more important, through redistributive taxation. This is an important consideration which has tended to be overlooked by the European beneficiaries of higher world interest rates in recent years.

A longer-term effect should not be neglected. The increased use of German savings in the United States rather than at home will have an adverse effect on the productivity of labour in Germany in the future, and thus lower the growth of German real wages in the future, at least pre-tax. As just noted, this could be offset by reduced taxation of wage-earners as increasing revenue is received from taxes on receipts of interest payments from the United States.

It turns out that there are numerous significant implications for Germany of the U.S. budget deficit. If we changed the name of the country to Brazil, or added Brazil as a third country, we could note that it may be a net debtor at floating interest rates and thus will lose from the higher interest rates on that account. Broadly we can say that in Germany and Brazil, producers in the tradable sectors may gain, in the non-tradable sectors may lose, new borrowers and net debtors may lose (unless the debts are longer-term at fixed interest rates), and new lenders and net creditors may gain, some persons and entities gaining from one point of view and losing from another.

I have been primarily concerned here with short- and medium-term considerations. But it has to be remembered that there are important longer-term effects of a U.S. deficit which is partly or wholly financed by lower U.S. and German investment, and which, in addition, must eventually lead to a reverse flow of funds to Germany. Even if the capital is not repaid, interest payments will steadily increase unless the deficit is reduced and eventually turned into a surplus. Leaving aside the complex implications of lower U.S. and German privately-owned capital stocks (relative to 'otherwise' levels), the presumption is that eventually there would have to be a real depreciation of the dollar to generate (or go with) the required non-interest current-account surplus. Therefore, many of the effects discussed here must eventually go into reverse. Furthermore, the expectation of such a reversal could affect current developments, including capital flows and the exchange rate. But let me return to short-term analysis now.

Is the U.S. Budget Deficit Expansionary or Contractionary for Germany?

So far I have simply assumed that the level of demand for German goods and services is successfully maintained constant by monetary policy. I have not asked whether, given a plausible policy reaction function and plausible wage behaviour, this would actually happen. On the one hand, it might be said that the depreciation of the D-Mark must be expansionary in its effects, since it shifts demand towards German goods and makes the export and import-competing industries more profitable. On the other hand, the higher interest rate will reduce investment and so have a contractionary effect. But if monetary policy and real wages are flexible, the net outcome of these two forces would not really matter, since a monetary policy change could offset the net effect, whichever way it goes.

The point to stress here is that, if we applied the Phillips-curve logic of the earlier analysis in this chapter, the net effect must be *contractionary*. The German terms of trade have worsened and the constant-employment real wage is likely to have fallen. This leaves aside sectoral considerations, since the equilibrium real wage in the tradables sectors may have risen and in non-tradables have fallen. Assuming a uniform wage-level throughout the economy the presumption (subject to numerous qualifications) is that the German short-term Phillips curve has shifted in an *adverse* direction, so that the optimal point chosen by the German authorities will involve both more inflation and less employment. Of course, if the real wage were completely rigid, the adverse effect on employment would be even clearer and would be quite independent of German monetary policy.

For the same reason the effect of a policy that leads to more capital inflow and hence dollar appreciation will be expansionary in the United States, essentially because it lowers the price-level for any given level of nominal wages and so shifts the U.S. Phillips curve in a favourable direction. This helps to explain how the United States managed to have a dramatic expansion in 1984 without any acceleration of inflation. But it must be added that one could construct a more complex model which focuses on sectoral effects, and causes the effect to be expansionary in the non-tradable sector in the United States and contractionary in the tradable-goods sectors, with an ambiguity about the net result. The same ambiguity (with sectoral effects in the opposite direction) could result for Germany.

Locomotive and Capital-Market Effects Combined

Packaging our two transmission processes together is easy and does not need to be spelt out in detail. A U.S. monetary expansion (with constant fiscal policy) would have a positive locomotive effect, so raising real output in the United States and thus depreciating the dollar and improving the German terms of trade (assuming that the *negative transmission* factors discussed earlier do not operate). At the same time it would lower the interest rate, draw capital out of the United States, and depreciate the dollar further, generating a U.S. current-account surplus and further improving the terms of trade of Germany.

The two transmission processes thus pull in the same direction in the case of monetary policy. Normally the capital-market effect works faster, often beginning even when a monetary-policy change is just anticipated or being initiated. This was the story of the monetary contractions of the United States and Britain in 1979 and 1980.

In the case of fiscal policy, the two transmission processes pull in opposite directions. The expansionary or locomotive effect of a U.S. budget deficit tends to *depreciate* the dollar and improve the terms of trade of other countries, while the capital-market effect tends to *appreciate* the dollar and worsen other countries' terms of trade. The greater the mobility of capital and the more expectational factors operate, the quicker the capital-market effect relative to the locomotive effect. Hence one might expect the dollar to appreciate at first, and to depreciate subsequently. On the other hand, if one takes the view that any Keynesian real-output effects will only be short-term, the locomotive effects will be gradually eroded.

Even though the locomotive effect of a fiscal expansion tends to depreciate the dollar and the capital-market effect to appreciate it, the two effects on Germany are not complete mirror images of each other. The reason is that the capital-market effect involves a German current-account surplus brought about by a shift of resources out of non-tradables into tradables, while the locomotive effect operates with current-account balance. The locomotive effect favours German export industries and hurts import-competing industries. The export industries benefit from the U.S. demand expansion and the import-competing industries lose from the German terms of trade improvement. German non-tradable industries benefit in so far as some part of the higher real incomes resulting from better German terms of trade and greater overall German expansion are spent on non-tradables. The capital-market effect involves a reduction in overall German spending and so clearly has an adverse effect on German non-tradables. On the other hand, the rise in the relative price of tradables to non-tradables will benefit both exportable producers *and import-competing industries*.

The Mundell–Fleming Model

One cannot pursue this subject without referring to the Mundell–Fleming model, and especially its two-country version owed to Mundell. This model, which ignores terms of trade and wages considerations but assumes perfect capital mobility, has dominated the analysis of the international transmission of disturbances through the capital market.

Its principal conclusions concerning the effects on Germany of U.S. expansion can be put quite simply. A fiscal expansion in the United States raises the world interest rate and appreciates the dollar. The dollar appreciation, being a D-Mark depreciation, raises demand for German goods and so is expansionary. On the other hand, the higher interest rate reduces German investment and is contractionary. Then the crucial assumption is made that *the nominal money supply in Germany is fixed*. German monetary policy is quite passive. Furthermore, fiscal policy does not change. In addition, the important assumption is made that the German price-level is constant. Thus it is the simplest kind of Keynesian model.

With the German demand for money depending on real income in Germany, on the price-level, and on the interest rate, and with the money supply fixed, the rise in the interest rate then requires a *rise* in German real income for the money market to stay in equilibrium. The exchange rate will depreciate sufficiently—i.e. capital will flow out sufficiently—to bring this about. It follows that the expansionary effect of the depreciation must outweigh the contractionary effect of the fall in investment. Fiscal expansion in the United States has then led to expansion in Germany, a case of *positive* transmission.

Similarly, one can analyse the effects on Germany of a U.S. monetary expansion. This time the interest rate falls and the D-Mark appreciates. Hence the demand for money must rise. Again, the exchange-rate effect must outweigh the investment effect, and the net result must this time be *contractionary*. Monetary expansion in the United States has then led to contraction in Germany, a case of *negative* transmission.

Even if we adhere to the crucial assumption of a constant nominal money supply, the certainties of these outcomes disappear completely once the model is modified in two plausible ways. Firstly, if the price-level of home-produced goods, rather than the average price-level, is fixed, a depreciation will raise the average price-level in Germany, hence increase the demand for money, and so reduce the need for a rise in real income when the interest rate increases. The opposite applies to an appreciation. It is surely reasonable to suppose that exchange-rate changes alter the price-level, and it is a flaw in the original model that this was ignored. Secondly, the depreciation will raise the nominal value of dollar-denominated bonds, and if positive stocks of these are held in Germany, it will raise nominal wealth and thus, probably, the demand for money on that account.

Another realistic complication that should be added is to allow for nominal wages to rise when the price-level rises because of the depreciation. The rise in wages will raise the prices of home-produced goods, raise the average price-level further, and hence increase the demand for money further. Therefore this effect will be deflationary, given that the nominal money supply is fixed.

The crucial limitations of the model is that it only tells us (subject to qualifications) what happens if the German money supply stays constant. It focuses on just one consideration, namely the effect on the demand for money in Germany of a change in the German interest rate that results from a monetary- or fiscal-policy change in the United States. It tells us nothing about likely German reactions in the form of monetary- or fiscal-policy changes. Why should the money supply stay constant? Perhaps the Mundell–Fleming analysis could be usefully reinterpreted as giving a guide to the direction in which German monetary policy must be adjusted to fulfil various possible German targets in response to shocks emanating from the United States.

German Policy Reactions[1]

Let us now look more closely at possible German policy reactions to a capital-market disturbance. We assume that there is a U.S. fiscal expansion combined with monetary contraction which raises the interest rate and depreciates the D-Mark. To start with I shall make the Keynesian assumption that the nominal wage in Germany is given (or changes only exogenously). This makes it possible to isolate some of the main considerations and to build on the simple Mundell–Fleming model. I shall allow later for nominal wage responsiveness to price changes.

I assumed earlier that, in response to the capital-market disturbances, Germany varies the money supply to keep employment constant. To achieve this, the *real* money supply has to fall because of the higher interest rate, but whether or not this requires a

[1] See the Appendix (p. 163 below) for a geometric exposition of the argument of this section.

rise or a fall in the *nominal* money supply depends on the size of the real money-supply fall that was brought about automatically by the real balance effect of the depreciation to which I have just referred. In other words, the impact effect (with a constant nominal money supply) of the capital market disturbances originating from the United States might be expansionary or contractionary, and this will determine whether the money supply needs to fall or rise to maintain the initial level of output.

So far we have one instrument (monetary policy) and one target (maintaining output or employment). But one could introduce at least one other instrument—German fiscal policy—and two more targets—namely restoring the real exchange rate and restoring the interest rate. Clearly, with two instruments and three targets it will not be possible to attain all the targets, and there are bound to be policy dilemmas. For example, a German monetary expansion would desirably lower the interest rate (not only in Germany, but also in the United States) and undesirably depreciate the D-Mark further. A German fiscal expansion would desirably appreciate the D-Mark (assuming that the capital market effect on the exchange rate outweighs the 'locomotive' effect) and undesirably raise the interest rate further. Much will hinge on the weight that is placed on the various targets.

Suppose we start in a situation where German monetary policy has restored the original level of output, and so attained one of the targets. But in the view of policy-makers the interest rate is too high and the D-Mark is too depreciated. If heavy weight is given to exchange rate stability—i.e. bringing about some D-Mark appreciation while maintaining employment without excess demand—the appropriate policy mix will consist of monetary contraction and fiscal expansion, which have offsetting effects on aggregate demand but both appreciate the D-Mark. This is, in fact, a mix that has been widely urged on Europeans and the Japanese as an appropriate response to the U.S. budget deficit. But fiscal expansion goes against their justified desires to reduce their own structural deficits. Hence short-term Keynesian and exchange-rate stabilization motives are in conflict with longer-term structural motives. More important, in the short-run this policy mix would raise interest rates further, an aspect that some of the advocates of this mix have failed to stress. It would be possible to engineer a fall in interest rates while maintaining employment with exactly the opposite policy mix: monetary expansion combined with fiscal contraction. But this would de-stabilize the exchange rate further.

Let us now introduce a nominal-wage reaction to the deprecia-tion. There will be no such reaction if fiscal expansion, monetary contraction, or both, prevented the depreciation completely. But if they do not, the rise in the domestic price-level is likely to lead to nominal-wage increases designed to restore, or at least move towards, the original real wage level.

The Phillips-curve assumption is that this attempt to restore real wages can be frustrated to some extent, possibly completely, by sufficient inflation of aggregate demand which causes prices to rise ahead of wages. If the original level of employment is to be maintained, and hence a lower level of real wages to be sustained, inflation must then rise. Governments will trade-off the extra inflation against the unemployment prevented, and will settle for some extra unemployment combined with some extra inflation. The higher unemployment may itself reduce the real-wage targets that trade unions aim for, which will thus moderate the nominal-wage increases and thus the inflation. In fact, with a sufficient reduction in aggregate demand initially it may be possible to achieve the lower level of real wages required without any continuous price and wage inflation. All of this means that the level of real demand and German output maintained in the new situation will be less than before the capital-market disturbance that started all this off. A disturbance that depreciates the D-Mark finally has a contractionary effect. This is the conclusion at which I arrived earlier.

The trade-off problem discussed above will still remain. Given aggregate demand policy, now determined by the exchange-rate outcome, there is still a trade-off between exchange-rate and interest-rate stabilization, the first requiring fiscal expansion and monetary contraction, and the latter the reverse. It need only be added that a principal reason, possibly the only reason, for trying to moderate or even avoid the depreciation is that, because of the wage reaction, the greater the depreciation the greater the unemployment that will finally result.

APPENDIX

POLICY RESPONSES TO A CAPITAL-MARKET DISTURBANCE

Figure 5 clarifies the policy dilemmas that arise for a country like Germany when reacting to a rise in the interest rate and depreciation of the D-Mark brought about by U.S. policies. The vertical axis shows an index of German fiscal policy, a movement upwards representing an expansion, while the horizontal axis shows an index of Germany monetary policy, a movement to the right being an expansion. The exchange rate is assumed to float and there is capital mobility. All curves are drawn on the assumption that the nominal wage is fixed in the period concerned.

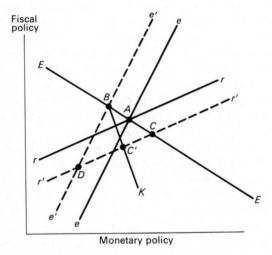

FIG 5

We are concerned with three targets, namely the exchange rate e (an increase being a D-Mark depreciation), the interest rate r, and the level of aggregate demand for German goods E (which determines employment). Thus there are two instruments and three targets. Monetary expansion raises e, lowers r, and raises E. Fiscal expansion raises r, raises E, and, in the diagram, is assumed to lower e.

We start at point *A*. This is the situation *after* the capital-market disturbance originating in the United States and *after* German monetary policy has been adjusted to restore the original (and target) level of German employment. The line (or curve) *EE* shows the combinations of the two policies that yield constant *E*, the line *ee* the combinations that yield constant *e*, and the line *rr* the combinations that yield constant *r*. In the diagram the plausible assumption is made that *ee* is steeper than *rr*, which means that fiscal policy relative to monetary policy has a lesser impact on *e* than on *r*. In the special case where fiscal policy does not affect the exchange rate at all (the locomotive effect just offsetting the capital-market effect) *ee* would be vertical. If a fiscal expansion actually depreciated the exchange rate, *e* would slope negatively.

A movement to the left of *ee* brings about appreciation. Points along the line *e'e'* would restore the exchange rate that existed before the capital-market disturbance. A movement to the right of *rr* would lower the interest rate, and points along *r'r'* would restore the interest rate that existed initially. Thus *EE*, *e'e'*, and *r'r'* represent the three targets.

Numerous policy implications can be read off the diagram. For example, employment can be maintained and the exchange rate restored at point *B*, i.e. by monetary contraction and fiscal expansion, while a movement in the opposite direction will restore the interest rate but increase the depreciation. If only monetary policy can be used not only would a change lead to a departure from the employment target (with a move to the right yielding excess demand) but there would be a conflict between moving towards *e'e'* and towards *r'r'*.

Both the exchange rate and the interest rate target could be attained at *D*. In that case the adverse effect of contractionary fiscal policy on the exchange rate would be more than offset by contractionary monetary policy, and the adverse effect of contractionary monetary policy on the interest rate more than offset by contractionary fiscal policy. But, of course, employment would be below target. If *ee* and *e'e'* were vertical or negatively-sloped (fiscal expansion causing *depreciation*) this conclusion would still apply. In the unlikely situation of *ee* being flatter than *rr* the two targets would be attained with expansionary policies(*D* being above *A*).

Let us now allow for a nominal wage reaction in the next period. Assume that the nominal wage reaction increases with the extent of depreciation and falls with the level of unemployment, being zero at *B*, where the original levels of the exchange rate and employment are attained. It is also zero everywhere along *BK*: as the exchange rate depreciates from its initial level an increasing level of unemployment is required to keep the nominal wage constant. Above *BK* the nominal wage rises, and below it, it falls. *BK* might be defined as the target demand line, rather than *EE*. If this target is to be attained, the policy choice has to be somewhere between *B* and *C'*.

REFERENCES

On the international transmission of disturbances, see in particular
M. Mussa, 'Macroeconomic Interdependence and the Exchange
Rate Regime', in R. Dornbusch and J. A. Frenkel (eds.), *International
Economic Policy: Theory and Evidence*, Johns Hopkins University Press,
Baltimore, 1979, and K. Hamada and M. Sakurai, 'International
Transmission of Stagflation under Fixed and Flexible Exchange
Rates', *Journal of Political Economy*, 89 (October 1978), 877–95. The
locomotive theory is discussed in G. E. Wood and N. A. Jianakoplos,
'Coordinated International Economic Expansion: Are Convoys or
Locomotives the Answer?', Federal Reserve Bank of St Louis,
Review, 60 (1978), 11–19.

For a detailed analysis of positive and negative transmission
through the terms of trade, see W. M. Corden and S. J. Turnovsky,
'Negative Transmission of Economic Expansion', *European Economic
Review*, 20 (June 1983), 289–310, and W. M. Corden, 'On Transmission and Coordination under Flexible Exchange Rates', in W. H.
Buiter and R. Marston (eds.), *The International Coordination of
Economic Policy*, Cambridge University Press, Cambridge, 1985.

The analysis of capital market transmission was pioneered in
R. A. Mundell, 'A Reply: Capital Mobility and Size', *Canadian
Journal of Economics and Political Science*, 30 (August 1964), 421–31
(which is the original reference for the two-country Mundell–
Fleming model). There is a very clear exposition in R. Dornbusch,
Open Economy Macroeconomics, Basic Books Inc., New York, 1980, of
the main Mundell–Fleming model and its two-country version. This
is further developed in R. Dornbusch, 'Flexible Exchange Rates and
Interdependence, *Staff Papers*, 30 (March 1983), 3–38, which
particularly emphasizes the nominal-wage response. For further
elaboration of this model, see W. H. Branson and W. H. Buiter,
'Monetary and Fiscal Policy with Flexible Exchange Rates', in J. S.
Bhandari and B. H. Putnam (eds.), *Economic Interdependence and
Flexible Exchange Rates*, M.I.T. Press, Cambridge, 1983.

International economic linkages are surveyed in F. Larsen, J.

Llewellyn, and S. Potter, 'International Economic Linkages', *O.E.C.D. Economic Studies*, 1 (Autumn 1983), (which emphasizes balance-of-payments constraints) and are discussed in various contributions in the book above edited by J. S. Bhandari and B. H. Putnam.

Finally, the interaction of monetary policies is analysed in a simulation model with a similar focus to that here, in J. R. Artus, 'Effects of United States Monetary Restraint on the DM/$ Exchange Rate and the German Economy', in J. F. O. Bilson and R. C. Marston (eds.), *Exchange Rate Theory and Practice*, University of Chicago Press, Chicago, 1984.

12

THE INTERNATIONAL MACRO-SYSTEM

IN this chapter I shall seek to assess the international macro-system that has emerged since the breakdown of Bretton Woods and the first oil shock. It is obvious that the system is unplanned and uncoordinated, and might be better described as a 'non-system'. But does it have some logic? We have seen in the previous chapter that, even with flexible exchange rates, the macro-economic policies of countries have overspill effects on other countries. The question then arises whether policies that take into account only the self-interest of countries should be modified to allow for international concerns. In the following chapter I shall pursue these matters further by considering the scope for the coordination of macro-economic policies.

The International Non-System

The principal feature of the present system is that it is a form of international *laissez-faire*. Not only does it allow free play to the private market, but it allows free play to governments and their central banks to conduct their macro-economic policies as they wish and to operate in the market as they choose. They are free to borrow and lend, and, above all, to intervene as they wish in the foreign-exchange market. With regard to exchange rates, they can choose any regime they wish. The essential feature of the present system is *decentralization* and absence of uniform, world-wide rules of any real significance.

The system naturally establishes an equilibrium. Indeed, this should not be surprising, since general equilibrium theory tells us that, given reasonable assumptions, decentralized decision-making with markets does tend to lead to an equilibrium. Looking first at aggregate demand policies, a change in one country's level of demand affects others through the terms of trade, and this is then likely to lead to adjustments of the others' policies, with possible feedback effects on the first. More interesting, perhaps, are the interactions through the capital market. As noted earlier in this book, in the main equilibrium has been established through U.S. 'benign neglect'. The United States has acted as the residual net buyer or seller of financial claims in the world capital market, and has tended to be passive in the foreign-exchange market.

Every other country can determine its own exchange rate relative to the dollar if it wishes, or, alternatively, can manipulate its exchange rate combined with monetary and fiscal policies to bring about a desired current-account outcome. But the United States stands by and lets things happen. Of course, this does not rule out some U.S. intervention in concert with other countries, nor U.S. pressure on other countries to intervene, the U.S. motive normally being *exchange-rate protection* (protection of her tradables sectors). This influenced the American advocacy of yen and D-Mark appreciation in 1977, and also played a part in the realignment of exchange rates forced by the United States in 1971.

Even when the United States does not intervene directly in the foreign-exchange market, the system is more symmetrical than might seem at first sight. The United States can influence the outcome through her (apparently) purely domestic monetary and fiscal policies, in which respect she is quite free, as free as all other countries. The mechanism of adjustment is primarily through effects on world interest rates. In a free-floating exchange-rate system a U.S. fiscal expansion, for example, will raise world interest rates, reduce investment in the United States and abroad, and, with constant fiscal- and monetary-policy stances in other countries, will produce a current-account deficit for the United States and, normally, appreciation of the dollar.

If other countries had fixed current-account targets they might engage in fiscal expansions themselves in response to the U.S. fiscal expansion. World interest rates would then rise further, but current-account imbalance and dollar appreciation could be avoided. In each country market forces would lead to a crowding-out of private investment by public borrowing. Alternatively, one might presume that market forces also influence government borrowing decisions: the higher real interest rates the greater the incentive to reduce borrowing. Thus, if foreign governments respond to market forces they will *not* aim to maintain current accounts constant when the U.S. government increases its borrowing, but will seek to have lower deficits or greater surpluses. Similarly, changes in U.S. monetary policy are likely to affect the value of the dollar and the U.S. current account.

Put in the most general terms, one can say that the problem is to reconcile the desires of different countries to buy and sell financial claims on the world market, the potential transactors including central banks that are intervening in the foreign-exchange market. The system will equilibrate if the demands or supplies of at least some of the transactors' financial claims are responsive to interest rates. Given some elasticity, price changes in this market can reconcile targets that initially seem incompatible.

It can be argued that the system is efficient for the same reasons that one usually regards a market system as efficient. Decentralized decision-making is more efficient and flexible than the alternative central-planning approach. Just as one presumes that households and firms normally know what is in their own interests—or are likely to know better than central planners—so individual governments are normally better judges than an international organization or committee of what would be an appropriate short-term trade-off point to choose, what the efficacy of various policy instruments are likely to be, how much the public sector should run into debt, and what political scope there is for various policy adjustments. The current *laissez-faire* international monetary system is simply a market system which co-ordinates the decentralized decisions reached by private *and public* actors and is likely to be as efficient in this as the market system is within the domestic economy.

We have thus a simple market paradigm—extended to include public actors, notably central banks—as a useful reference point for analysing the system. But we know that markets do not inevitably lead to optimal results. There are income distribution considerations, externalities, public goods, information problems, and monopolistic distortions and oligopolistic (strategic) interactions. In an environment where there is a limited number of very large actors the possibility of oligopoly and the need for the ideas of game theory are very relevant. Clearly these issues cannot be pursued thoroughly here—though they are currently an agenda for research—but some of them underlie the discussion to follow in this and the next chapter.

I now leave these generalities to turn to some more specific matters.

Are Current-Account Imbalances Undesirable?

In the light of this discussion it is worth analysing more fully the continuous concern with current-account imbalances. By 1978 the O.P.E.C. current-account surplus had practically disappeared but major imbalances within the O.E.C.D. had emerged. In particular, there were large U.S. current-account deficits and Japanese surpluses in 1977 and 1978. Much concern was expressed about these imbalances. European politicians and commentators reprimanded the Americans for their high deficit, Americans reprimanded the Japanese for their surplus, and the U.S. government put pressure on the Japanese government to take steps to reduce the surplus.

But why the fuss? One could put a simple argument (to be qualified below) that there was no cause for concern. Japan was importing financial assets and the U.S. was exporting them. Japan had switched, at the margin and (as it appeared with hindsight) for a short period, from importing goods to importing financial assets. Provided the private and public decision-makers in each country knew what they were doing, why should an increased exchange of financial assets for goods have been undesirable? Presumably there are gains from trade, including trade which involves financial assets.

The first qualification must be that the level of this trade depends partly on the level of public sales of financial assets—i.e. on the two budget deficits. For example, the Japanese budget deficit was very high in 1978, but not quite high enough to offset the Japanese private-sector financial surplus. If it had been even higher, Japan as a nation might have become a net seller of assets. Two views could now be taken. One is that the two countries' budget deficits were not necessarily at the optimal levels from the national points of view, and hence it cannot be said that the net trade in financial assets that resulted was necessarily optimal. Alternatively, it might be argued that each country could be assumed to maximize some kind of national social-welfare function leading, among other things, to particular budget deficits. Given its domestic policy choices, free trade, including trade in financial assets, is then optimal.

The second qualification is that the net national trade in financial assets also depends on the *private* financial balances in the two countries, and these may be non-optimal.

The private financial balance depends on savings and investment. Considering savings first, the very high Japanese and the very low U.S. household savings ratios reflected private decisions about the desirable ratios of wealth to income. If it is granted that in general households are the best judges of their own interests, why should their savings decisions be excluded from this presumption? The qualification is that fiscal policy may distort savings decisions. Fiscal policy in the U.S. tends to discourage savings and in Japan to encourage it. Hence, in the language of trade theory, there is a 'domestic distortion' which leads to non-optimal trade. On the other hand, from an international point of view it can be argued that each government is entitled to its own view about optimal fiscal policy, its tax system reflecting an implicit social-welfare function. Given this, free trade becomes optimal. Furthermore, while Japanese subsidization of savings may be non-optimal for Japan, it need not have an adverse effect on the United States.

Turning to private investment, unusually low investment in Japan and high investment in the United States resulted (among other things) from different monetary policies, these in turn reflecting different views about the Phillips-curve trade-off. The fear of inflation was certainly greater in Japan than in the United States. Again, it can be argued that these policies, while not necessarily optimal, reflected national attitudes and policy judgements. Each country should be entitled to make its own macro-economic policy choices.

Having said all this, one might ask why, nevertheless, Americans and Europeans objected to a Japanese surplus. Two answers might be given.

(1) The problem may have been not the Japanese surplus but rather one of its proximate causes, the large rise in the volume of Japanese exports. This adversely affected industries around the world which competed with Japanese exports. This adverse effect would have largely remained even if the whole of the extra Japanese export income had been spent on extra imports (rather than leading to a surplus), given that the beneficiaries of the extra import demand would have been different from the losers from Japanese export expansion.

Significant reductions in sectional incomes or expectations of such reductions tend to create a sense of crisis. When Japan exports more goods and imports more financial assets there are a variety of sectional income effects in the United States. The most obvious one is the adverse effect on competing tradable-goods producers, which may lead to strong pressures for protection. Since the financial-asset price will tend to rise (the interest rate to fall) buyers of these assets will also lose. On the other hand, producers of non-tradables and sellers of financial assets will gain. But the American gainers—such as borrowers in the housing market or firms supplying investment goods—are unlikely to attribute their gains to an increased Japanese willingness to save.

(2) The concern may be with the uncertainty and potential instability of the situation. It is realized that a large current-account surplus is unlikely to last. The accumulation of financial assets by the Japanese and of financial liabilities by the Americans may to some extent be a portfolio adjustment (e.g. a shift out of financial into real assets by U.S. householders) and to some extent a reflection of short-term monetary policies. In any case, it may be felt that it is not sustainable.

Eventually the expectation of yen appreciation owing to the Japanese accumulation of dollars generated speculative capital inflows and the appreciation became difficult to resist. But the associated dollar depreciation was widely regarded as undesirable. This seems a little puzzling. After all, it only tended to reverse the loss of competitiveness of U.S. import-competing industries that had earlier taken place. Perhaps the explanation is that dollar depreciation also carried with it losers—notably the foreign holders of dollars, not to speak of direct and indirect consumers of imports in the United States—and brought with it fears that it was not just a once-for-all adjustment but rather was a harbinger of exchange-rate instability.

To summarize, large current-account imbalances usually generate expectations of exchange-rate changes. Any large exchange-rate change, whether actual or prospective, is usually considered a problem (i) because it is bound to have adverse effects on some groups, and (ii) because it generates fears of exchange-rate instability.

The U.S. Budget Deficit

Similar issues arise in connection with the U.S. budget deficit which began to be significant from 1982 and is growing in size as a proportion of U.S. gross national product.

In 1984 neither the U.S. budget deficit in relation to G.N.P. nor government interest payments, were dramatically higher than in many other O.E.C.D. countries, though the U.S. relative position had certainly changed. A comparison with Japan is particularly instructive. In 1979 the U.S. government was in small surplus, and by 1984 its deficit was 3.8 per cent of G.N.P. At the same time the Japanese deficit fell from 4.8 per cent of G.N.P. in 1979 to 3.1 per cent in 1984. But the U.S. public debt in relation to G.N.P. is still well below that of many other O.E.C.D. countries, including Japan. The perceived problems are really three.

Firstly, the swing into deficit has undoubtedly been a factor in the appreciation of the dollar, and one perceived problem is that this could be sharply reversed. Possibly the expectation of the growing deficit has been as important as the actual deficit in explaining the appreciation. Because of the size of the U.S. economy the swing in her budgetary position over a short period undoubtedly makes a big impact on the world capital market. The counterpart of the budget deficit has been a current-account deficit (reinforced by the revival in U.S. investment demand) of truly impressive proportions. The current-account deficit was about $6 billion in 1982 and in 1984 was expected to be $68 billion (greater, for example, than the $58 billion deficit of all developing countries). There are statistical problems which suggest that all world current-account deficits are being overstated considerably, but it does seem that the United States has a growing deficit which cannot go on indefinitely.

The essential argument which underlines concern or doomsaying about the U.S. budget and current-account deficits is that these deficits represent a stock adjustment, and the time must come when the world's savers will be increasingly reluctant to put indefinitely increasing shares of their portfolios into U.S. Treasury Bills. And as the turn-around approaches—indeed, once it is clearly foreseen— the dollar will sharply depreciate. The U.S. may continue to absorb a large flow of funds, but it will have to do so by paying even higher interest rates, and with a depreciated dollar.

The U.S. exchange rate is clearly equilibrating the market, taking into account demands and supplies generated by expectations that seem quite reasonable. It is not a 'disequilibrum rate'. The concern is that the market equilibrium rate will change dramatically, and, as always, the concern is for the dislocation of trade, for factoral income distribution, and, in this case, above all for inflationary pressures in the United States, that would result. *Changes* in exchange rates, rather than *levels*, are feared—often feared excessively. Considering the levels, presumably a dollar depreciation would have some beneficial effects, reversing certain of the adverse effects of the appreciation.

The second problem is that the deficit must have contributed to the rise in world real interest rates, with adverse effects on developing countries. It is true that fiscal contraction in Europe and Japan had an offsetting effect by lowering interest rates, and until 1982 the rise in interest rates must have been caused primarily by the monetary contraction policies followed in the major O.E.C.D. countries. But a reduction in the deficit would no doubt lower world interest rates, with beneficial effects on major borrowers among the developing countries.

In terms of the analytical framework presented earlier one could argue that the market is efficient when it uses the interest rate to ration out scarce funds, and the rise in the interest rate has then 'efficiently' crowded-out developing-country borrowers when demand from the U.S. Treasury increases. But while the market outcome may be 'efficient' it is nevertheless not 'optimal' because it ignores income-distribution considerations. Thus a special concern with effects on developing countries can be fitted into a framework which uses the market paradigm as a starting point but also takes into account the standard qualifications from welfare economics concerned in this case with international income distribution.

The third problem resulting from the U.S. deficit and the associated real appreciation is the decline in profitability and employment in the tradable-goods sectors in the United States. This has led to increased protectionist pressures in the United States. This aspect has motivated some economists in the United States to advocate measures to bring down the dollar urgently (a form of *exchange-rate protection*). But it has to be added that the obverse effect has been some decline in protection in Japan—though not, it must be noted, in Europe.

Macro-Economic Policies and the International Interest

In a market system the participants naturally modify their actions to take into account the actions of others. But they do so only in their own interests and do not explicitly take into account the interests of their neighbours. The need for the participants to take into account explicitly the interests of others, possibly as part of a system of formal co-operation, arises when there are oligopolistic elements in the market and when changes have to be made in large discrete steps rather than in the form of marginal, and flexible, adjustments. Before considering the scope for policy co-ordination or co-operation in more detail it is thus necessary to review the nature of the favourable or unfavourable effects that countries spread around them as a result of their macro-economic policies. The discussion of the transmission of disturbances in the previous chapter was purely positive. My concern is now with the normative implications of the transmission of disturbances, and of the various possible policy responses.

To begin with, *shocks* must be regarded as undesirable in their international effects. I have in mind here sudden and relatively unexpected policy changes that have large effects. Other things being equal, countries should discourage each other from imposing such surprises on one another. Of course changes are rarely fully unexpected, particularly when they emerge from the democratic process. But a big policy switch which is never seen as certain to come until close to the time when it actually happens, and the consquences of which cannot always be foreseen, must be regarded as having, at the mildest, some adverse effects. Examples are the shift in U.S. monetary policy at the end of 1979 and the shift in U.S. fiscal policy associated with President Reagan's election (though it must be remembered that the 1979 shift to money targeting in the United States had the approval of other major O.E.C.D. governments).

Leaving aside its domestic effects, such a shock presents two problems for other countries. Firstly, it brings about sectoral redistributions, where the effects on losers are always seen (for political reasons or because of adjustment difficulties) as more important than the effects on gainers. I have already stressed this. The second problem is that these policy shifts require policy reactions from other countries, reactions which usually take time and which may be difficult to implement because of policy rigidities. The monetary-policy reaction from Germany, for example, to a U.S. fiscal-policy switch must be regarded as part of the German adjustment process. The less warning Germany has, the bigger the losses that will be imposed on her as a result of her being temporarily *not* on the optimal point of the new short-term Phillips curve generated by the U.S. policy change.

One might wonder whether the United States presents a special problem because of her economic size. Is she an exceptional generator of shocks for other countries? There have certainly been some major U.S. policy switches, firstly the change from excessive expansion in 1976–8 to severe contraction from 1979, and then the remarkable fiscal policy shift. Many other countries, notably Britain and France, have displayed similar policy instabilities, but they do not present major problems for other countries when they shift gear on their own. Only when several major European countries and Japan shift gear together can the effects be as great as when the United States does. The danger is thus in synchronization, which can result from common shifts in intellectual fashions, possibly encouraged by the considerable extent of high-level contact and information exchange among O.E.C.D. policy-makers that now exists. I shall return to the issue of synchronization versus policy divergences again in the next chapter.

Leaving aside shocks, it is by no means obvious in which direction countries should urge each other with regard to their macro-economic policies. In other words, even if they agreed to co-operate—to take each others' interests into account in formulating their own policies—it is by no means obvious what the co-operation should consist of, other than to discourage shocks. Let me explore this further with regard to (1) aggregate-demand (locomotive) policy, and (2) capital-market (borrowing and lending) policy, the distinction between (1) and (2) being the same as that made in the previous chapter.

(1) In a two-country model with positive transmission it is clear that in the short run one country (the United States) benefits the other (Germany) the more it expands demand. The short-term output and income increases in the United States improve Germany's terms of trade, which is a benefit in itself and may lead to additional employment gains in Germany through the short-term Phillips-curve mechanism outlined in the previous chapter. With a flexible exchange rate Germany can insulate herself from the higher inflation that economic expansion will bring in the United States, losing only later when the United States contracts in order to slow up the inflation.

Once we go beyond two countries the matter is not so straight-forward. As discussed in the previous chapter, U.S. expansion is likely to have positive transmission effects for commodity exporters, including most developing countries, by improving their terms of trade, but may have negative transmission effects for competitive industrial countries, who may lose more from higher commodity prices than they gain from better markets in the United States.

(2) At a time of high interest rates and the developing-country debt crisis one is bound to conclude that, other things being equal (i.e. with aggregate demand held constant), the more countries seek to lend and the less they seek to borrow the better for the rest of the world. Thus, the more they reduce their budget deficits while compensating with monetary expansion, the better. In doing so, not only do they bring down interest rates and ease the debtors' problems (as well as the problems of the private banks), but by depreciating their own exchange rates they also improve other countries' terms of trade, with the usual Phillips-curve benefits. Thus the fiscal contractions of Japan, Germany, and Britain since 1979 should be viewed with some favour from an international point of view, even though Japan's policies were often criticized from outside because of the exchange-rate impact.

Yet the emphasis on lowering interest rates is not the complete story. The view that interest-rate reductions are desirable reflects a bias in favour of debtors. There are also gainers from high interest rates, namely creditors (assuming they expect the debts owed to them to be honoured) and current savers. But the bias in favour of debtors may at present be justified when one takes into account the international income-distribution considerations mentioned above.

Furthermore, I have referred to the criticism directed at Japan for the consequences of her high savings and lending, as reflected in her current-account surpluses. A country that allows its real exchange rate to depreciate—which is part of the equilibrium process of transferring savings to the rest of the world—is not always thought to be benefiting the rest of the world, essentially because of the adverse effects on tradable goods producers in competing countries. In terms of the implicit social-welfare function of many governments —a function which places heavy weight on these sectoral effects—it is by no means clear in which direction governments would wish to push each others' interest-rate policies.

REFERENCES

The argument that the international 'non-system' has a logic and that the principles of welfare economics are appropriate for assessing it, is more fully developed in W. M. Corden, 'The Logic of the International Monetary Non-System', in F. Machlup *et al.* (eds.), *Reflections on a Troubled World Economy*, Macmillan, London, 1983. For an earlier scepticism about concern with current-account imbalances, see J. Salop and E. Spittaller, 'Why does the Current Account Matter', *Staff Papers*, 27 (March 1980), 101–34.

This chapter and the previous one do not deal with short-term exchange rate determination, and the relationship between short-term and longer-term exchange rates—subjects that are highly relevant for an understanding of the current system. There is a very large literature in this field. An up-to-date book with many relevant contributions is J. F. O. Bilson and R. C. Marston (eds.), *Exchange Rate Theory and Practice*, University of Chicago Press, Chicago, 1984. See especially the survey paper by Mussa, 'The Theory of Exchange Rate Determination', Branson's contribution, 'Exchange Rate Policy after a Decade of "Floating" ', and 'Exchange Market Intervention Operations: Their Role in Financial Policy and their Effects' by Henderson.

This chapter, like the next one, touches on a wide range of international economic issues. Basic sources of information are the *World Economic Outlook* and the *Annual Reports*, published by the International Monetary Fund, and the *Annual Reports* of the Bank for International Settlements. See also the biannual *Economic Outlook* of the O.E.C.D. All these give accounts of exchange rate, capital market, and current-account developments. See also many articles in the Brookings Papers on Economic Activity, and in particular P. Hooper, 'International Repercussions of the U.S. Budget Deficit', *Brookings Papers on Economic Activity*, 2 (1984).

13

MACRO-ECONOMIC POLICY CO-ORDINATION

THERE are several conceivable levels of co-ordination among major O.E.C.D. countries. I shall review four of them in this chapter, beginning with the most ambitious and least realistic and ending with the two that are already practised. But first, something must be said about the desirability of policy synchronization.

Is Policy Synchronization Desirable?

Suppose we take the view that it is in the international interest to keep key variables in the world economy—aggregate demand, the terms of trade of developing countries, real exchange rates, real interest rates, and so on—as stable as possible, letting them change only where required as part of the normal process of 'stable, non-inflationary growth'. What does this imply for the co-ordination of macro-economic policies?

The central issue is that divergent policies among the major O.E.C.D. countries *destabilize* real exchange rates while tending to *stabilize* real interest rates, aggregate demand for the O.E.C.D. area as a whole, and hence the terms of trade of developing countries. Thus monetary expansion in the United States combined with monetary contraction in Europe and Japan will depreciate the dollar but have offsetting effects on commodity prices and interest rates. Similarly, fiscal expansion in the United States combined with fiscal contraction in Europe and Japan (broadly, the situation from 1982 to 1985) appreciates the dollar but tends to stabilize O.E.C.D. demand and world interest rates. Given a positive-demand (loco-motive) shock emanating from the United States, reactive demand expansion in Europe will tend to stabilize the exchange rate (and the U.S.–Europe terms of trade), but destabilize total O.E.C.D. demand, and hence relative commodity prices. Similarly, given a capital-market shock coming from the United States in the form of higher interest rates and increased borrowing owing to, say, a greater fiscal deficit, a fiscal expansion in Europe (combined with monetary contraction) will stabilize the exchange rate, but de-stabilize the interest rate. There is thus a dilemma as to what are desirable reactive policies in the international interest, given that shocks emanate from the United States, or possibly from one or more other major economies.

The solution appears to be to have synchronized *non-shock* policies. This would require policy co-ordination of a high degree, and involves difficulties and objections which I shall discuss below. Here it must be noted that policy synchronization as such—i.e. without avoiding unstable policies—can do more harm than good. There have been at least three synchronized policy episodes post-war. The first was in the late nineteen sixties, leading to a general acceleration of inflation from 1968. For the nine largest O.E.C.D. economies together, the fiscal impulse in 1967 was the largest in any year from 1965 to 1976. The second was the overheating of 1972 and 1973. All the major O.E.C.D. countries followed expansionary monetary and fiscal policies in that period, and the speed of the expansion that resulted was exceptional. As discussed in Chapter 6, this episode could be regarded as having originated in the United States, with the reactions of other countries being inevitable, given the (more or less) fixed exchange-rate system until March 1973. But the 1972–3 inflationary outburst is certainly a warning against the dangers of synchronization. Finally, the unexpectedly severe world recession of 1980 to 1982 must be regarded as having been caused by the synchronized tight monetary policies of the United States, Japan, Germany, Britain, and Canada from 1979 to 1981.

Fully Co-ordinated Policy Synchronization

An extreme form of co-ordination would involve full policy synchronization. The aim would be to stabilize real exchange rates without destabilizing interest rates, levels of aggregate demand, and the terms of trade. Broadly, countries would move together in their macro-economic demand management policies, and also in any switches in their policy mixes: thus, when it is thought desirable to stimulate employment there might be co-ordinated fiscal expansions. There would, presumably, be steady and moderate monetary targets.

The obvious problem is that the needs and economic philosophies of different countries do not always coincide. A fiscal expansion desirable for one country may be regarded as too inflationary for another. This, of course, is the central argument for the decentralized decision-making that is the characteristic of the current non-system. Countries have *policy independence* even though real effects are transmitted from country to country so that there is also *interdependence*. The argument against policy co-ordination of this kind is really the same as the standard argument against monetary integration. It hinges on the fact that monetary policy, like fiscal policy, does have real effects, though possibly only in the short-run. Hence *policy independence is desirable and interdependence is inevitable.*

If monetary policy had only nominal effects, flexible exchange rates could really insulate economies from the effects of each others' monetary policies, yet allowing each country to have its own chosen inflation rate. But when monetary policies have no real effects then presumably they do not matter anyway, and there is no point in having a system which allows countries to have different monetary policies. The classic case for flexible exchange rates was certainly based on the assumption that monetary policies did matter, so that there was some value in giving countries monetary independence.

Quite apart from this argument in favour of policy independence, there are two other difficulties in the way of full policy co-ordination. Firstly, there is the purely organizational problem. Unless a philosophy of 'hands-off' monetary targeting is accepted, goverments want to be able to adjust policies quickly in response to changing circumstances, and co-ordination of policies by sovereign governments is likely to involve delays. Secondly, as I have observed earlier, overall stability may be less likely when O.E.C.D. macro-economic policy is centralized, possibly moving massively one way or another in response to intellectual fashions, than when it is decentralized, different countries being perhaps in different phases of the political or intellectual fashion cycle.

Mutual Policy Adjustment

In the second level of co-ordination countries seek to modify each others' macro-economic policies to take some account of each others' interests. The aim is not to synchronize policies, or to stabilize nominal or real exchange rates, but, less ambitiously, to bias each country's policies in a direction more favourable to its neighbours.

The underlying theory behind this approach is that, in the small-numbers case, a non-coordinated equilibrium which is the outcome of the *laissez-faire* system is not likely to be Pareto-efficient. There exist sets of policies that could make all countries better off. This is best explained in terms of the simple two-country locomotive model sketched out in the previous chapter. Each country's expansion would improve the terms of trade of the other, so that it 'loses' some of the gains from its expansion. If each country chose its policies on the assumption that the others' policies are given—i.e. if it perceived a given Phillips curve as the outcome of the other's policies, and then optimized subject to that—a Nash equilibrium would result. In taking into account the adverse effects of expansion on its terms of trade a country is behaving rather like a monopolist. Both countries could then be better off if they *both* expanded more, each benefiting through the terms of trade from the expansion of the other. Co-operative equilibria can dominate the outcome from plausible non-cooperative games.

Here again there are several difficulties or objections.

The first is that co-operation is difficult to achieve. It is also a sort of game. But, presumably, it is the task of diplomacy to extract some benefits from the existence of potential mutual gains.

The second difficulty is that a principal aim of co-ordination relates to aggregate demand (locomotive) policies which are only concerned with short-term Keynesian effects, given that the fundamental neo-classical factors—in particular, real wages relative to labour productivity—determine employment in the medium run. Yet the processes of policy co-ordination, even in the modest form of mutual policy adjustments attained by negotiations, take time, during which the circumstances that gave rise to the negotiaitons will have changed. Specifically, the short-term Phillips curve will have changed.

A third difficulty or objection that has been advanced concerns the inflationary bias of government policies. It will hardly be disputed that politicians' interests do not necessarily coincide with the national interest. It could be argued that politicians generally take a short-term view, aiming, above all, to win the next election. Since the favourable output and employment-increasing effects of expansionary policies tend to come ahead of the unfavourable inflationary consequences, the politicians will be predisposed to excessive expansion from the point of view of the true national interests. Suppose now that positive transmission applies. The Nash equilibrium will then involve less expansion than a co-operative solution which maximizes the joint interests of politicians. But the deflationary bias of the Nash solution may simply offset the inflationary bias of the politicians, so that the net effect of co-operation may not be favourable from the point of view of the true long-term national interests.

How much weight should one give to this argument? There are plenty of countries and historical episodes where one can find evidence for an inflationary bias in the political process. But the recent recession, which was induced by the considerable enthusiasm of major governments for halting inflation, gives no support at all for the generalization.

The final difficulty is more basic. As pointed out at length earlier, it is by no means clear in which direction countries should push each others' macro-economic policies. There are conflicting targets. In the case of the locomotive issue, there are both positive and negative transmission effects to allow for, and in the case of capital-market (borrowing) policies exchange-rate protection, Phillips-curve effects, and interest-rate targets send out different signals.

It is worth looking more closely at the possible outcome of non-coordinated policies in the capital market. Because of varying objectives and decentralized decision-making even within countries it is by no means clear in which direction the system is biased relative to a solution efficient for the world as a whole. Let me be somewhat theoretical for the moment, and suppose that countries were not concerned with Phillips-curve or exchange-rate protection motives, and ignore the sectoral pressure-group effects on fiscal policies. Let us assume that governments only take into account the normal optimal borrowing and lending considerations, and in addition wish to improve their terms of trade in financial assets. Debtor countries would want low interest rates and creditor countries high interest rates. Thus debtor countries would tend to restrict their borrowings, so as to reduce interest rates, and creditor countries would seek to restrict their lending. The Nash equilibrium would lead to less trade (trade of financial assets for goods) than would a Pareto-efficient co-operative solution. The argument is the same as that advanced earlier with regard to the locomotive theory.

For the creditor country, some of the gains from extra lending would be 'lost' in the form of lower interest rates.

Suppose, further, that fiscal policy is the relevant policy instrument in both countries. Then decentralization would lead to excessive fiscal expansion, and hence less national lending abroad, in a creditor country like Japan, and excessive fiscal contraction, and hence less borrowing, in a debtor country.

These considerations may motivate fiscal policies of countries that are close to credit-worthiness constraints, so that increased borrowing has marked effects on the interest rates they have to pay. In the case of the major O.E.C.D. countries, one has to ask whether the borrowing of their governments is likely to make a big difference to the particular interest rates they pay—i.e. whether there are significant risk premiums differentiating returns on bonds denominated in different currencies—and whether their borrowing is likely to affect the overall structure of world interest rates. So far it is not apparent that the fiscal-policy decisions of the United States have been much influenced by this endogenous interest-rate effect, but the situation might well change. In addition, governments do not normally concern themselves with the collective interests of private creditors, so that, in creditor countries, it is improbable that fiscal policies will be expansionary in order to raise world interest rates for the benefit of these creditors.

Co-ordination of Exchange-Market Intervention

The third level of co-ordination, namely in the foreign-exchange market, is by central banks and takes place continuously, though, as I shall show, in indirect form.

First, something must be said in general about the logic of direct intervention in the foreign-exchange market. This time the different countries' monetary and fiscal policies are taken as given, being uncoordinated. These 'fundamentals', though themselves changeable, will have certain exchange-rate outcomes which intervention policy cannot alter, other than in the very short run. But, superimposed on the exchange-rate effects of the underlying policies are the portfolio shifts of market participants based on expectations about these policies and other events in the future, and on varying assessments of exchange risk. It is well-known that short-term exchange rates are primarily determined in asset markets, and that market participants react rapidly to the continuing flow of 'news', continually reassessing the likelihood of interest-rate and exchange-rate changes in the future. The expectations-induced portfolio shifts bring about variations in current exchange rates.

Some people hold the view that such shifts are often based on false models, false news, foolish analysis of correct news, bandwagon effects, and so on. It is implicit in this view that the market participants are likely, on average, to make losses, and that intervention designed to be stabilizing, which is based on correct models, wise analysis of news, and so on, must be profitable. Given that the portfolio shifts are usually out of one interest-bearing asset into another, and not into or out of money, intervention which is meant to offset these shifts should be sterilized: it should change the relative supplies of the relevant bonds, supplying more bonds of the kind required and less of the kind that market participants wish to move out of, and should therefore not change money supplies. The real part of the economy will then be insulated from these purely financial effects.

The important qualification to this view is that some portfolio shifts by market participants may be based on sensible assessments of news, and may have reasonable chances of being profitable. If dollar bonds look safer than before relative to D-Mark bonds, or if the D-Mark is expected to depreciate, it may be wise not just for the market participants but for the nation as a whole to move marginally out of D-Mark bonds. There is then no justification for intervention. It will not be stabilizing, even though it may be 'leaning against the wind', and, in addition, it will be loss-making for the central banks that intervene. Why should it be in the public interest—as distinct from the interests of the sectors that gain from the exchange-rate effect—to have a loss-making central bank?

It follows that the case for this kind of sterilized intervention must rest on a reasonable belief that the central bank does have better information or, more likely, a superior capacity for analysing existing information—often a matter of judgement—than the very short-term-orientated market participants. In my view, this is often quite likely, but it is well to be aware that this is the requirement.

Let us now grant that, at least at times when the market seems to go a little 'haywire', there is a case for central-bank intervention. The further issue then arises whether it need be 'co-ordinated'?

Clearly, any one central bank can intervene provided it has the resources to do so. Nevertheless, it is accepted that co-ordination between central banks is desirable. There are two reasons.

Firstly, intervention, like any economic activity, involves risks. There may be a high chance that it will be profitable, but there *is* also the risk of loss. After all, the bank is pitting its judgement against speculators who have every incentive to use their money profitably. So central banks wish to spread the risk. Secondly, a central bank has limited resources of foreign currency, so it may not be able to achieve its objectives on its own, and, if this is known, 'credibility' is lost, and the amount of intervention required to attain a given exchange-rate result will increase. Clearly, this is not a problem if the Bundesbank wishes the depreciate the D-Mark, in which case it will accumulate dollars, but it is a problem if it aims at appreciation. The problem will be solved if the Bundesbank has access to funds from the Federal Reserve.

The current situation is that the Federal Reserve rarely intervenes in the foreign-exchange market itself. It leaves intervention to other central banks. Nevertheless, there is close co-operation between the major central banks. Firstly, those that are active in the market do not intervene at cross-purposes: one central bank does not try to push a currency up while another tries to push the same currency down. In a true *laissez-faire* system this would be a possibility, but central banks do co-operate. Secondly, it can be observed from actual behaviour that central banks intervene only by 'leaning against the wind'—i.e. by slowing-up market forces, rather then preventing them altogether or even reversing their effect. They have followed the I.M.F.'s guidelines for floating in the sense that they do not intervene 'aggressively', i.e. reverse the direction in which a rate is moving. Thirdly, mutual credit arrangements among the major central banks play an important role.

The Federal Reserve swap network is a system of mutual credit facilities between the Federal Reserve and fourteen other central banks and the Bank for International Settlements. Other central banks that wish to intervene in the foreign-exchange market draw dollars to finance their intervention, and on the few occasions when the Federal Reserve wishes to intervene it can draw on foreign exchange through this network, since it does not hold any significant foreign-currency balances. Since such drawings are not automatic, but imply approval of the purposes to which the funds are put, it follows that intervention, though apparently by only one central bank, is really co-operative.

Exchange of Information

The final and most modest level of co-ordination is information exchange about macro-economic policy intentions. This goes on all the time, primarily under the auspices of O.E.C.D., but also through numerous other channels. Exchanging information must surely be good, since it is better to make decisions on good information than bad. Governments and central banks need to know not only what others are planning to do but also how others would react to their own policy changes. With advance information of neighbours' changes in policies, countries can more readily make appropriate adjustments. Nevertheless, there have been times, as in 1980 and 1981, when policy switches of countries coincided, and it appears that they did not take full account of the total effect of the whole herd reversing direction together.

It should not be thought that 'information exchange' can fully avoid shocks and their adverse consequences. Politicians and officials of a country often have no more knowledge well in advance of what policy changes there will be—changes that are usually the outcome of a complex political or bureaucratic negotiating process, if not dependent on elections or various unexpected exogenous events—than have outsiders. There is also the uncertainty of how the domestic economy will respond to known policy changes. At O.E.C.D. meetings they can only convey their uncertainties.

Given how little policy-makers may know, it is improbable that they would practise strategic behaviour and spread false information. But it is worth noting that, in theory at least, there can be an incentive to do so. Consider again our simple locomotive model where the United States benefits Germany the more the United States expands, and the more she does, the more Germany will expand, this, in turn, benefiting the United States. It will then pay the United States to make Germany believe that she will expand more than she actually intends, since the German response will be beneficial for the United States. If there were negative transmission it would also pay the United States to convey this expansionist impression. In response Germany would then expand *less* (her Phillips curve being expected by her to move in an adverse direction), this, in turn, benefiting the United States.

Conclusion

In the previous chapter I have referred to the numerous concerns produced by variations in exchange rates that are, in turn, explained by monetary and fiscal policies. The fact is that we have an international *laissez-faire* 'non-system', and exchange rates reconcile the divergent policies and circumstances of countries. There are complaints when the dollar appreciates and when it depreciates, or even when it is just expected to depreciate. The fact is that all changes generate gainers and losers, and the focus is always on the adverse effects.

It was always an illusion to think that the highly desirable *policy independence* that flexible exchange rates make possible must imply absence of *policy interdependence*. Monetary policies, fiscal policies, and exchange rates have *real* effects, and that is why they matter. Incidentally, even if nominal money-supply policies and nominal exchange-rate changes had no *real* effects, other than in a very short period, because of the rapid adjustment of nominal wages, fiscal policies would still have real efects, producing either real exchange-rate changes or unemployment even when nominal exchange rates are fixed. While the international *laissez-faire* system may not be perfectly Pareto-efficient, so that there is certainly some scope for intelligent co-ordination, as discussed in this chapter, it does bring about outcomes that reflect the divergent tastes—in policy choices, in savings habits, and so on—of various countries. That refers particularly to the Japan–U.S. current-account 'imbalances'.

The biggest problems have come from the shocks to the system that are generated by big, sudden, and sometimes synchronized policy changes in major countries, and by expectational instabilities reflected in exchange-rate variations caused by policy uncertainties. The most recent example is the policy of monetary contraction which was pursued rather suddenly—for some good anti-inflationary reasons and in response to the second oil shock—by five major O.E.C.D. countries from 1979. This policy reduced the demands for the developing countries' exports and raised real interest rates, hence producing the debt crisis. No doubt this crisis would have developed in any case, though on a much lower scale, because of unwise lending and poor use of funds, but certainly not so suddenly.

The policy of monetary contraction was imposed under the inspiration of monetarism, and it certainly had the desired effect of sharply reducing inflation after a short lag. Because the deflation was relatively greater in the United States and Britain it also helps to explain the appreciations of the dollar and sterling. But the outcome of the deflation of 1979 to 1982 bears out the arguments for gradualism and steady policies that Milton Friedman, the father of monetarism, taught us many years ago. Inevitably, credibility of governments with regard to their new monetary-policy firmness could not be fully established, so that expectations were slow to adjust. As always, the shocks to the system have come from governments. This is not surprising when they are the largest actors in the system.

REFERENCES

Theoretical work on macro-economic policy co-ordination and strategic interdependence is currently booming. Many of the issues are surveyed in R. N. Cooper, 'Economic Interdependence and Coordination of Economic Policies', in R. W. Jones and P. B. Kenen (eds.), *Handbook of International Economics, Vol. II*, North-Holland, Amsterdam, 1985, and an important article, containing some empirical work, is G. Oudiz and J. Sachs, 'Macroeconomic Policy Coordination among the Industrial Economies', *Brookings Papers on Economic Activity*, 1 (1984), 1–75. Some of the discussion in this chapter is based on W. M. Corden, 'Macroeconomic Policy Interaction under Flexible Exchange Rates: A Two-Country Model', *Economica* 52 (February 1985), which contains a more rigorous and fuller development of various arguments.

See also R. C. Bryant, *Money and Monetary Policy in Interdependent Nations*, The Brookings Institution, Washington, 1980; various contributions to W. H. Buiter and R. C. Marston (eds.), *International Economic Poicy Coordination*, Cambridge University Press, Cambridge, 1985; and J. Sachs, 'International Economic Policy Coordination in a Dynamic Macroeconomic Model', National Bureau of Economic Research, Inc., *Working Papers*, No. 1166, Cambridge, 1983.

Pioneering work on international macro-economic policy interaction and strategic behaviour was done by Hamada in K. Hamada, 'A Strategic Analysis of Monetary Interdependence', *Journal of Political Economy*, 84 (August 1976), 677–700, and elsewhere. A recent paper, K. Hamada, 'Strategic Aspects of International Fiscal Interdependence, Univ. of Tokyo, mimeo, 1984, analyses interaction in the capital market in a two-country model, along the lines briefly presented in this chapter.

An account both of synchronized policy episodes and of several short-lived attempts by individual countries to 'buck the trend' (expand more or contract less than other countries) is given in F. Larsen, J. Llewellyn, and S. Potter, 'International Economic Linkages', *O.E.C.D. Economic Studies*, 1 (Autumn 1983).

INDEX OF NAMES

SUBJECT INDEX